STAMPS
AND STAMP
COLLECTING

CHANCELLOR
PRESS

STAMPS
AND STAMP
COLLECTING

FRANTIŠEK ŠVARC

CHANCELLOR
PRESS

First published in Great Britain in 1993
Designed and produced by Aventinum
for Chancellor Press,
an imprint of Reed Consumer Books Limited,
Michelin House, 81 Fulham Road, London SW3 6RB
and Auckland, Melbourne, Singapore and Toronto

Copyright © 1993 Aventinum, Prague
Copyright © This edition by Reed International
Books Limited 1993
Translated by Alena Linhartová
Illustrations by Spytimír Bursík, Gustav Krum,
Václav Kubela, Zdena Marschallová, Pavel Sivko,
Michal Skalník, Evžen Urban, Jaroslav Velc
Photographs by Marie Bonaventurová, Adolf
Burger, Richard Pfleger, Jindřich Richter,
Jaroslav Sýbek
Graphic design by Václav Konečný

ISBN 1-85152-288-3

A CIP catalogue record for this book is available
at the British Library

Printed in the Czech Republic by Svoboda, Prague
1/22/08/51-01

Acknowledgements

The Publishers would like to thank the following
individuals and institutions for providing the
pictorial material used in this book:
František Švarc, Ladislav Dvořáček, Zdeněk
Hrnčíř, Josef Sůva, Vladimír Viklický
and Severin Zrubec
Postal museum, Stockholm
Gesellschaft für deutsche Postgeschichte,
Frankfurt am Main
Union philatélique de Genève
Technisches Museum, Wien
Union Postale Universelle, Bern
SPADEM, Paris

Contents

Introduction

We do not know precisely when people began to collect things as a hobby. The word 'collection' appears in a speech made in the year 66 BC by Cicero (106—43 BC), the Roman orator, statesman, and philosopher. Besides writing and giving speeches, Cicero was also a collector of manuscripts and works of art.

Johann Wolfgang von Goethe (1749—1832), the famous German poet, once remarked that collectors were happy people, who devoted their free time to a world of their own creation. While Goethe himself did not collect stamps — they did not exist in his lifetime — he did, however, collect minerals.

An Italian stamp depicting Marcus Tullius Cicero.

The collection and study of postagestamps became popular in the second half of the 19th century, and soon came to be called 'philately' from the Greek *ateleia*, meaning 'exempt from payment'.

Nowadays, philately includes collecting items other than just stamps that are of philatelic interest, such as postmarks and postal stationery (for example, stationery with an imprinted postage stamp, and postal labels). All over the world, stamps and stamp collecting have become a life-long hobby, providing hours of enjoyment.

Millions of people have been and are interested in stamps and

Above, clockwise from top left: Russian stamp depicting I. P. Pavlov; Italian stamp depicting Enrico Caruso; Monaco stamp depicting Franklin D. Roosevelt; Finnish stamp depicting Mauno Koivisto; Indian stamp depicting Jawaharlal Nehru. *Below:* An Italian stamp depicting Albert Einstein.

stamp collecting. Among them have been some very famous celebrities and personalities, such as the Russian physiologist I. P. Pavlov (1849—1936), the excellent Italian tenor Enrico Caruso (1889—1921), the American President Franklin Delano Roosevelt (1882—1945), and the Indian statesman Jawaharlal Nehru (1889—1964). The Finnish President Mauno Koivisto (b. 1923) was even awarded a medal for his stamp collection, entitled 'The Working-class Movement in Finland'. The Austrian composer Robert Stolz (1880—1975) was a stamp collector, too; he composed, among others, a 'Philatelic Waltz'! The famous German physicist Albert Einstein (1879—1955) said that collecting stamps was especially useful for intellectuals and academics since, in his view, collecting was an extremely valuabie form of recreation and relaxation.

Stamps are also admired by people who are not collectors, but make up a large proportion of visitors to postage-stamp exhibitions. Even specialist exhibitions are well attended by the general public.

A record sleeve of Robert Stolz's 'Philatelic Waltz'.

A hall of philately exhibits.

1 *A Survey of Postal History*

Early Forms of Communication

Postal history is linked closely with the history of human society. From its very beginnings, it is likely that mankind felt a strong desire to exchange knowledge and information. The earliest peoples probably felt the need to communicate with one another in the course of their work, or when battling against the elements. The way in which they communicated eventually evolved into what we today call speech. Soon these early races learned how to share their knowledge, information, and emotions; they learned how to pass on news. Initially this was done through spoken words, but later it became possible to communicate over ever increasing distances by the use of messengers. The messenger would have to memorize the message, and then repeat it to the person for whom it was intended. Other means of conveying messages evolved as well, such as sound signals (shouting), and lighting signals (fire, smoke). These signals, however, were not always reliable, and were not as effective as using a messenger.

The foundation of writing led to the use of stone and clay tablets in Assyria from about 3000 to 1000 BC as means of conveying messages. Later, more suitable materials appeared and were in common use — papyrus, leather, parchment, cloth, and, finally, paper — and the transfer of messages took the form of certain postal links.

The communication of written information is illustrated in a number of ancient Egyptian wall paintings from about 1200 BC. Papyrus was used by the Greeks and the Romans until AD 600. In pre-Christian times, wax tablets, or *codicilli*, as well as wood shavings, were used by the Romans. The Greeks used animal skins, which eventually gave rise to the use of parchment made of tanned calf, goat, or sheep skin. Parchment was widely used in Europe from the 6th to the 15th century.

Nearly all of the ancient cultures about which we have more detailed knowledge sent messages by foot, by equestrian couriers, or by messengers. They travelled along the routes traditionally called 'ways', which were also used for the movement of large armies and for transporting military equipment. These routes also allowed for the collecting of taxes, and enabled rulers to control their territories.

The use of pedestrians and runners by those in power to deliver messages is not a recent one. In ancient times, a ruler would receive written dispatches, brought every morning by messengers, who sometimes had to cover great distances without any relief. This would demonstrate that these communications must have been well established from the earliest times.

Trade was also used for communicating information. The

Homer, the earliest Greek epic poet and the reputed author of *The Iliad* and *The Odyssey*.

An ancient Greek vase. The upper part of the vase depicts King Proetus handing inscribed tablets to Bellerophon, who is to deliver them to the king's father-in-law, Iobates.

earliest form of trade was probably a type of bartering that took place among traders or merchants. Because these merchants travelled extensively, they became the first people to bring messages over great distances. In this way, their roles as traders and communicators became one.

Ancient Egypt and Babylon

A form of postal communication existed in Ancient Egypt during the reign of the Fourth Dynasty (c. 2600–2500 BC) pharaohs. Pedestrian and equestrian couriers, travelling along the military routes to Libya, Ethiopia, and Arabia, were provided with accommodation by the local inhabitants. The pharaoh only released certain towns from this duty as favour.

The pharaoh's messengers had a difficult and dangerous job: during their travels they might be threatened by wild animals, and,

on occasions, by enemy spies wishing to capture military secrets. In addition to the perils of his journey, there was also the real possibility that the pharaoh might punish the messengers for any bad news that they carried. It is not surprising that messengers would appoint guardians for their children before setting out on such a journey, and that Egyptian scholars living in the period of the Twelfth Dynasty would advise their male offspring to choose any occupation other than that of messenger!

In Babylon during the reign of Hammurabi (c. 1900 BC) there was also a form of postal communication. Hammurabi's 'Code of Law' mentions parcels, and something similar to postal orders. It is evident from the clay tablets preserved in the archives belonging to the governor of Larsa that Hammurabi also kept up an extensive correspondence with his governors and officials.

A copy of an ancient Egyptian wall-painting portraying a messenger handing a communication to an Egyptian minister.

Assyria and Persia

It is well documented that there was regular and uninterrupted postal activity in Assyria. Numerous documents have been preserved from the vast library of the Assyrian ruler Assur-bani-pal, who ruled between the years 668 and 626 BC. His library was excavated in Nineveh, the capital of ancient Assyria, in the second half of the 19th century. When the ancient cuneiform script was deciphered, and Assyriologists were able to begin to understand the library's contents, they learned that Assur-bani-pal had ordered copies made of all ancient literary works. In this way his library preserved evidence of the most important events in the life of Ancient Babylon and Assyria, including an extensive knowledge of grammar, medicine, and the classification of animals, plants and minerals. In addition to this important historical information, the library contained letters written by military commanders and officials to Assur-bani-pal, his mother, his son

A Roman legion on the move.

and daughter, and to the members of the Assyrian nobility.

The cuneiform script used in Assyria at the time was engraved with a sharp stylus on a wet clay tablet. The tablet was then dried in the sun; if a letter was particularly important, and contained information that was to be preserved for a longer period, then the tablet was fired in a kiln. These tablets — the equivalent of our letters — were usually put into clay 'sleeves', to preserve the privacy of the correspondence. The name of the addressee was engraved on the sleeve, and the sender would occasionally close it with his personal seal.

The method of communicating messages was very sophisticated in Ancient Persia. The Greek historian and philosopher Xenophon (c. 430 — c. 355 BC), writing about the foundation of postal communications by the Persian king Cyrus the Great, who ruled between 559 and 530 BC, considered this to be a very important step because of the size of the Persian Empire. In order to discover what was happening in the remotest parts of his kingdom, the king first demanded that the distance that could be covered reasonably in a day by a messenger on horseback be calculated. Next, staging posts equipped with men and horses were established at regular intervals along the route. At each staging post, an official was responsible for the receipt of letters and their onward journey by providing messengers on fresh horses; the official also looked after tired messengers and their horses. This service was carried out round the clock, as night messengers were substituted for the daily couriers, and vice versa.

This smoothly orchestrated postal service was restricted to the so-called 'Royal Route', which stretched for 2,500 kilometres from Sardis, the capital of Cyrus's empire, to Sus, the winter residence of the Persian kings. There were 111 staging posts on this route, and it took a messenger ninety days to cover the entire distance on foot, while a mounted messenger was able to complete the journey in five to seven days. To provide for speedy dispatches, every one or two kilometres messengers on horseback were positioned who would relay the message until it reached its destination. This 'fast post' could reach the capital from the remotest parts of the kingdom in two to three days. This is perhaps why the Greeks used to say that the Persian king would sit comfortably at his table while feasting on fresh fish caught in the Aegean Sea.

A copy of an ancient Egyptian wall-painting from a Theban tomb portraying the handing of a message to the pharaoh.

A chariot on the bronze palace doors at Balavat (Assyria).

Ancient Greece

The peculiar administration of Ancient Greece was also reflected in its postal communications. Greece in the 8th century BC did not consist of a single political entity, but of a number of small city-states. Because the borders of the individual city-states were not set far apart, there was no regular organized postal service. If a military or any other important communication had to be dispatched, either a ship was sent (in the case of the islands or of the numerous Greek colonies on the Black Sea and Mediterranean coasts), or a messenger was dispatched on foot.

Being a messenger in Ancient Greece was considered to be an honourable and responsible duty; often the winners of the Olympic Games were selected for this office. The messages sent usually concerned commercial, political, and military affairs. Messengers who used to deliver messages over short distances were called *gramatoforos* (comparable to today's postmen), while *hemerodromos*, or daily runners, served on long distances.

The difference between celebrated winners of the Olympic Games and professional messengers is not completely clear, and it is little wonder that the names of many famous *hemero-*

A scene from Assur-bani-pal's lion hunt. A drawing based on an alabaster relief discovered on the walls of the Royal Palace at Nineveh.

A clay 'sleeve' with a clay tablet letter.

involved in other tasks, such as measuring road distances and constructing roads. For example, the Greek running champion Deinosthenes worked as a road engineer.

The Greeks had a special way of protecting the secrecy of their messages: first they took a long wooden stick, ensuring it was of uniform thickness, which they then cut in half. A military commander would carry one half of the stick with him on his journey, while the other half was left at home. If the commander decided to send a message, a leather strip, known as a *skytale*, was wound in a spiral fashion around his half of the stick. The message was then written across the *skytale*. The leather strip was unwound and sent home by a messenger. The recipient would wind the message on his half of the stick, which would enable him to read it. However, the secret message could be breached if anyone intercepting the message had a stick of compatible thickness around which to wind the *skytale*, and therefore to decipher the message.

Ancient Rome

The conveying of messages reached its peak with the Romans, who had an advanced and well-organized transport system that provided reliable connections with the individual Roman provinces. These covered vast territories, ranging from the Middle East to Britain in an east-west direction, and from the Crimea in the north to Gibraltar and North Africa in the south.

Even before the foundation of the Roman Empire, the gover-

dromos have been preserved to the present day. For example, the runner Euchidas was sent to Delphi to fetch the sacred Olympic flame after the Battle of Salamis. He covered the distance of 1,000 *stadia* (one *stadium* is about 183 metres) in a day, and subsequently died of exhaustion. It is also known that when the Persian king Darius (521–486 BC) waged war against Greeks in 490 BC, the Athenians dispatched the runner Pheidippides to seek help from the Laconians; he covered the distance of 1,200 *stadia* (225 kilometres) in a day and a night. Olympic messengers were often nors of the individual provinces used special couriers for official dispatches. However, travel was rather slow in those days, and the routine conveying of messages was a tedious business. For some reason, speedier horseback messengers rarely were used.

There was a significant improvement in communications after the fall of the Roman Republic, during the reign of the first Roman Emperor Augustus (27 BC–AD 14). At that time, postal communication was called *cursus publicus* ('public post'). It conveyed messages, persons and their luggage, and was run by specially appointed officials and servants. The name 'public post' was not wholly accurate, since in the beginning it did not serve the public but was used only for imperial and governmental purposes. Only after some time did it become available to wider cross-

sections of free Roman citizens, who had to pay for the service. The term *cursus publicus* later gave rise to the naming of postal communications in Spanish (*correo*), Catalan (*correu*), and Portuguese (*correio*).

Cursus publicus consisted of a network of two kinds of centres: the so-called *mansiones* and the *mutationes*. *Mansiones* were staging-posts that provided resting places at regular intervals of a day's journey. In addition to replacing tired horses, messengers, drivers, and carriages, these staging-posts also provided accommodation and food for travellers and postal personnel. Between each resting stage there were usually six or seven smaller relay staging-posts — the *mutationes* — where, again fresh horses could be substituted for tired ones.

It was this system of interconnected travel that gave rise to

the word 'post'. Rest and relay staging-posts did not have special names of their own, but were designated as follows: *mansio posita in . . .*, or *mutatio posita in . . .*, literally translated meaning 'a post situated in . . .' The Latin word *posita,* 'situated', or 'established' gradually gave rise to the expression 'post', which entered into common usage in other European languages around the 13th century.

These postal services were based on a sophisticated network of roads that connected Rome with its provinces. From the establishment of the Republic in 510 BC, the Romans built roads that connected Rome with its important Italian regions. The Roman roads were sophisticated for their time, the quality of which can be confirmed by the fact that a number of them have partially survived to the present day.

A Persian 'Royal Route'.

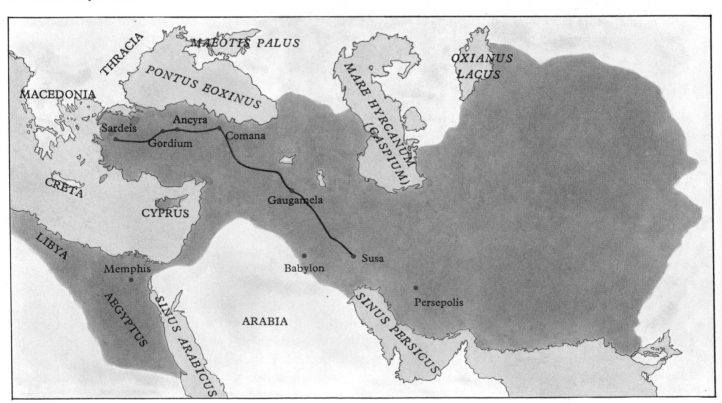

A secret Greek message.

The effort put by the Romans into the construction of their roads can be understood in terms of the roads' strategic importance. The highways were paved; the major roads were up to ten metres wide, and minor roads were four to seven metres wide. The highways were usually named after the officials who had been entrusted with their construction. The Appian Way, which was twenty metres wide in some places, ran from Rome to Capua, and was later extended to Tarentum and Brundisium. The Aurelian Way connected Rome with Liguria; the Valerian Way ran from Rome to Aternum; the Flavinian Way connected Rome with Ariminium, and was linked to the Via Aemilia, which led from Ariminium to Placentia.

The roads had milestones that showed the distance either in miles or in feet. In the centre of Rome stood a gilded column (*milliarium aureum*), which represented the centre of the Roman road network. On the column were inscribed the distances of important places from Rome.

Post was carried by messengers on foot and on horseback. The messengers on horseback transported both passengers and goods in addition to carrying letters. They had at their disposal several kinds of coach, from a light, two-wheeled carriage, to a heavy, four-wheeled wagon which was drawn by eight to ten horses, mules, donkeys, or oxen.

The establishment and operation of such postal communication was expensive. The cost was not, however, borne by the Imperial treasury, but by communities situated close to the roads. They were obliged to provide the wagons, horses, and coachmen free of charge, as well as providing food and fodder. It is therefore little wonder that many families moved to other settlements where such obligations did not exist. The extent of this burden can be judged by the fact that when the Emperor

During the reign of the Emperor Augustus, Roman streets, squares, and temples were decorated with numerous statues of Roman heroes, and also with statues of the emperor himself.

Roman postal communications — *cursus publicus.*

Nerva (AD 96—98) temporarily abolished this duty to maintain the running of the state postal services, the Roman senate minted special commemorative coins to mark the event.

While the Roman organization of postal services was very advanced, because it was concerned principally with transporting persons and their luggage, and not with the conveying of messages, we should not overestimate its importance in terms of the development of the postal system.

The Fall of the Roman Empire

In AD 395 the Roman Empire was divided into two independent parts — western and eastern — with Rome and Constantinople as their respective capitals. The year 476, when the Roman mercenary armies deposed the last Roman Emperor Romulus Augustulus, is generally considered to be the year when the western Roman Empire fell. And with its destruction came the collapse of its advanced state postal system.

In several administrations following the fall of the Empire, postal organization was based on the previous Roman system. These included the reign of the Ostrogoth king Theodoric the Great (AD 493–526) in Italy, and the kingdom of the Vandals, which was situated in modern Tunisia and Algeria between AD 429 and AD 534. The Frankish Empire, which was established in Galicia in the 5th century, preserved the *cursus publicus* almost in its original form. This is evident from the complaints raised in a time when the last Roman soldier had long been gone. Those complaining were forced to bear the costs of maintaining the roads and operating postal services. Their burden was even greater than in Roman times because in addition to the emperor, nobles were given permission to use these postal roads. Indeed, there were quite a few services. One permit, called *tractoria* and which is preserved to this day, lists in detail what the staging post was obliged to provide for the courier and his entourage: horses, forage, wood, candles and torches; beef, pork, mutton, lamb, and plenty of bread; beer, wine, bacon, vinegar, and various spices; geese, pheasants, chickens and eggs, salt, almond and honey — are all included.

The great King Charlemagne (AD 768—814, crowned Holy Roman Emperor in AD 800) improved information links and established regular postal communications in his Empire. These ran from the town of Autissiodurum (present-day Auxerre, southwest of Paris) to southern France, Spain and Italy; and through Aachen to central and southern Germany. The death of the son of Charlemagne, Louis the Pious (AD 814—840), followed by the division of the Frankish Empire in AD 843, led to the extinction of this postal system.

The Arab Empire

In addition to the postal system of the Frankish Empire, another well-functioning postal service appeared in the early Middle Ages. It was founded in the Middle East, in the Arab Empire, under the Abbasid dynasty of caliphs, who ruled from Baghdad between AD 749 and 1258.

This was a huge empire, extending from India to Spain and from Arabia to Armenia. From

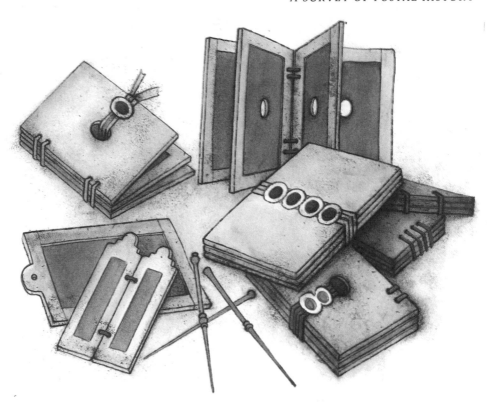

Letters written on wax tablets, which were used in Ancient Rome.

The Appian Way.

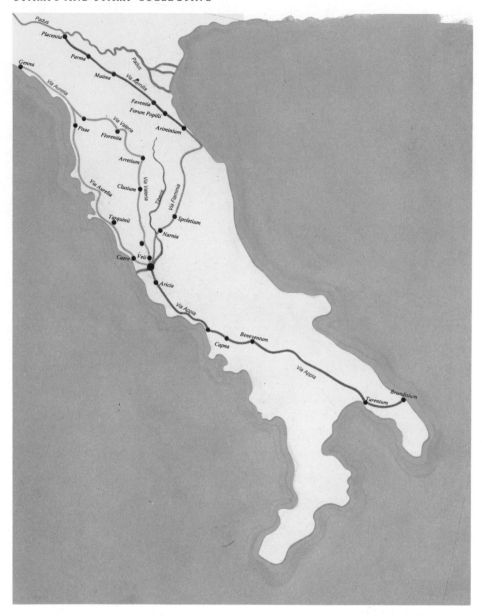

The Roman road network.

Roman milestones. Their size can be compared with a human figure.

Baghdad, the seat of the caliphs, six great roads originated. Every two miles on the road there was a staging-post. Because some of these posts were situated at great distances from bigger towns, or were even in desolate regions, wells had to be sunk, and food and supplies for messengers had to be grown or assembled. Postal transport was provided by couriers on foot, or by riders on camels, horses, or mules. Detailed records were maintained of letters and consignments received or dispatched.

The head of this postal system was the master of the posts, who was based in Baghdad. All regional staging-postmasters were subject to his authority; they themselves had the power to enforce the punctuality of couriers as decreed, and to punish any unjustified delays.

One example of how highly the caliphs regarded this central post office is shown by a statement of Caliph al-Mansura, who ruled between AD 754 and AD 775: 'My throne rests on four columns, and my power rests on four men — on a reputable Judge, on an efficient Director of Police, on an honest Finance Minister, and on a reliable Master of the Posts, who informs me of everything.'

The postal system was constructed and administered strictly in accordance with its Roman model, however, unlike the Roman system, the costs of its maintenance and operation were borne by the caliphs.

The political decline of the Abbasid Empire in the second half of the 9th century unfortunately brought with it the end of this excellent postal institution.

An Austrian stamp depicting a Roman postal coach.

Above: A bronze sestertium — the Emperor Nerva's commemorative coin.

A messenger hands over a sealed letter to Charlemagne. A picture from 'Chronique de France' (15th century).

An Austrian stamp depicting an emperor's messenger.

The Middle Ages

After the fall of the western Roman Empire, with certain exceptions most rulers lost interest in the carrying of messages, persons, and their luggage, which they left to other departments and agencies. It was only with the development of trade and the spread of education that an increasing interest in a properly established postal system, accessible to the wider public, resulted in the foundation of courier associations, or agencies.

Merchants' associations operated a system of special postal couriers or messengers, or mercantile post, which served long routes, for example from Hamburg to Venice, from Antwerp to Vienna, from Nuremberg to Wroclaw. Larger towns along these routes functioned as staging-posts, where couriers could be exchanged.

Because the highways were not considered safe at that time, couriers were issued with a letter of safe conduct by the nobleman through whose estates the postal route ran. The nobleman might even provide a special escort, for which the nobleman was paid a fee. Every firm of merchants that was a member of a postal association had the right to send parcels up to a certain weight free of charge. Letters could also be sent by individuals, or by non-member firms of merchants upon the payment of a fee.

Monastic posts were another form of postal communication. Manuscripts and written records from the 11th century show that bishoprics and monasteries had full-time, salaried couriers who ensured postal links; individual religious orders also were interested in these communications. However, it was not easy to maintain these links because of the great distances between the monasteries that proliferated throughout France, Italy, Spain, and Germany. Reliable couriers

A monastic messenger.

Municipal messengers dressed in summer and winter clothing from Hanau, a German town.

had to be sent for, and thus these lengthy journeys were generally undertaken by the monks themselves, with paid messengers being dispatched over shorter distances. Mendicant friars, who were numerous in the Middle Ages, were also used as couriers.

During the Middle Ages, universities such as those at Paris, Bologna, Naples, and Prague were in regular contact with one another. This led eventually to the establishment of well-organized university posts. The university students were interested in such links because parcels from home could be delivered reliably, even over long distances. At the beginning of the 15th century, the University of Vienna dispatched messengers to Wroclaw, Leipzig, Nuremberg, Prague, and other centres of learning.

The most important post, which for a period seriously rivalled the Royal French Post, was that of the Sorbonne. Students at this Parisian university were divided into four groups: French, English, German, and Norman. Each national group administered and operated its own couriers, who swore an oath of loyalty. The fees that were collected from conveying messages were used to pay the courier, and the balance went into the coffers of the respective student body.

Major towns where trade flourished set up their own municipal posts, and they were followed by the smaller towns. While the municipal post did not deliver parcels and letters inside the town, it operated links with other, even distant, towns. Initially the post mainly employed foot messengers, but in the 13th century it began to use coaches as well. The quality of service provided can be understood from the following example: in the mid-13th century, the Barcelonian Municipal Council introduced a surcharge for the delivery of 'express and privileged letters'; if such a letter was misplaced, the Council was obliged to compensate for its loss, which was similar to the refund provided with today's registered post.

In this period of flourishing postal communications, Nuremberg had over 200 messengers, and, in the 14th century, Leipzig had postal links with Augsburg, Magdeburg, Brunswick, and Hamburg, among others, which themselves had postal links with other towns. Hanseatic towns (Hanse was a commercial league of Germanic towns in what is today northern Germany, Poland,

Holy See and various ecclesiastical dignitaries, as well maintaining links with foreign rulers and scholars. Later, when the Order became more influential, it established numerous and often distant networks, and it became necessary to hold regular assemblies. The head of the Knights' excellent postal service was the postmaster general, who set up his headquarters in Malbork, as well as the seat of the Grand Master of the Order. The Teutonic Knights used young couriers on horseback, who were selected from the servants of the Order. The so-called *vithings* were free yeomen who, after proving their allegiance, joined the Order once it colonized the Baltic lands east of Germany. The *vithings* were employed to carry important and urgent dispatches. Later, this

An 'express' municipal messenger (16th century).

and the Baltic states) also had postal links, which were the best known and lengthiest of all.

Staging-posts — what we today would call post offices — were often situated in town halls. Each town had a couriers' guild, and messengers would wear the livery and coats-of-arms of their respective towns, which signified their office; they would also be armed with a spear. Each courier or messenger had a book in which he would note the departure and arrival times of each journey he made, from which his wage was calculated.

Individual chivalric orders also had their own messengers. The Teutonic Knights, for example, established a very advanced postal communication system. One reason for this was the need to be in regular contact with the

Malbork, a 13th-century castle in the Gdansk region (Poland), formerly the seat of the Order of Teutonic Knights.

A postal horn from the first half of the 19th century.

A French post office from the reign of Louis XV.

postal organization also delivered private letters, for which they charged a fee. When the Order of the Teutonic Knights was dissolved at the beginning of the 16th century, it spelled the end of its postal network.

The butchers' post spread principally throughout Germany, and was in operation in some places until the early 19th century. Butchers, who had their own transport and travelled widely to purchase their meat, were well suited to operate a postal service, especially between remoter communities. Local authorities would make and sign special contracts with the butchers' guilds to carry letters, parcels, and persons. The butcher was either paid a special fee, or was exempt from local taxes. To mark his arrival, the butcher would sound a horn; this may well have been the origin of the posthorn.

The Late Middle Ages

In addition to private postal services, a regular state post existed in France in the 15th century. In 1464 King Louis XI (1461—1483) established the royal post. This was based partially on the Roman model previously described. Staging-posts were established every seven kilometres along all the military roads, and each post was administered by a postmaster. The postmaster was obliged to have at his disposal four or five

A post office from the 17th century.

fresh horses at all times, which he, personally, would use for the swift transport of royal dispatches. The postmaster also supervised a larger number of mounted couriers. The royal post was used by the king, state envoys, and papal couriers. The king could grant special permission for individuals to use the royal post; they were, however, expected to pay six *sous* for the privilege of using horses between any two staging-posts.

In the 16th century the French royal post was made available to the public in order to increase its profitability. For a while there were two rival postal services operating in France: the royal post and the Sorbonne post. When the royal post became available to the public, the Sorbonne post gradually lost its importance, and was finally abolished at the beginning of the 18th century.

The postal system in England developed independently and separately from those on the European continent. At first, messages were conveyed on foot and by mounted couriers. Regular links were established only in exceptional circumstances, for example during the War of the Roses (1455—1485). King Henry VIII (1509—1547) improved the entire postal network; however, although he appointed a master of the posts to head the service in 1516, this appointment did not really improve the English post in any significant way.

In addition to the royal post, some short-lived private posts operated in England. Because the royal post did not provide links with the Continent, foreign merchants who were resident in London were forced to establish their own post, headed by one of their own number. During the reign of James I (1603–1625), even this merchants' post was administered by the master of the posts.

As late as the second half of the 17th century, a regular state post was set up in tsarist Russia. Previously, a service called *Jam* had been in operation. The word *jam* probably was derived from the Tartar word *dzjam*, which translates as 'a staging post'. *Jam* was used to transport passengers and diplomatic messages only when required, rather than on a strictly regular basis.

2 The Introduction of Postage Stamps

The Thurn-Taxis Family

There were thus four major factors that contributed to the establishment of regular postal communications in Europe: the foundation and growth of European towns; the development of crafts and trades, with their associated crafts' and merchants' guilds; the development of mercantile relations and the establishment of banks; and, finally, the important geographic discoveries of the 15th and 16th centuries, which resulted in the conquest and exploitation of new territories.

The requirements of trade and diplomacy in 15th-century Italy gave rise to courier links that could be considered the origin of the present-day postal system. Many couriers who were employed principally by the Papal Curia — the governmental departments of the Vatican — belonged to the Taxis family.

King Maximilian I (1486–1519, crowned Holy Roman Emperor in 1493) borrowed from the experience provided by this Italian courier network.

Maximilian married the French princess Mary of Burgundy in 1477, and became the ruler of a vast empire that included Austria, Germany, the Netherlands, and a large part of Italy. Because it was necessary to convey messages regularly and safely throughout these territories, in 1488, Maximilian and Frederick III (1440—1493, crowned Holy Roman Emperor in 1452) met Janetto von Taxis at Innsbruck, where the three signed an agreement regarding the foundation of 'postal routes', or regular postal communications. Janetto von Taxis was appointed Master of the Posts. As stated in a town chronicle of Memmingen in 1490, regular postal communications were established linking Austria and Holland, and France and Rome, by order of the German King Maximilian I.

Later, Maximilian's son Philip the Beautiful (1482—1506) appointed Franz von Taxis as Master of the Posts in March 1500. Five years later, they signed and agreement under which Franz von Taxis established and operated postal communications linking the Netherlands, where the King had his court, and the French and Spanish royal courts, for which he was paid an annual fee of £ 12,000. In this way, Franz von Taxis became the founder of the Thurn-Taxis post. The post rivalled all other private mails, and became prominent because it enjoyed the patronage of the court.

The Taxis family established

**Maximilian I,
the Holy Roman Emperor.**

staging-posts along the roads, where fresh horses could be substituted for tired ones. In larger towns they appointed local administrators, who received and distributed parcels or letters, and operated strict postal timetables. The Taxis gradually extended postal communication outside the Empire; this was used primarily to convey the emperor's private correspondence. However, as early as the beginning of the 16th century, individual letters from the public were also being delivered.

The Taxis family received a large income from these postal communications, and it is therefore little wonder that they kept them successfully under their personal control.

The Emperor Ferdinand II (1617—1637, crowned king of Bohemia in 1617, king of Hungary in 1618, and Holy Roman Emperor in 1619) appointed Leonard von Taxis as Master General of the Posts (*Generaloberpostmeister*) in 1595.

During the Thirty Years' War (1618–1648) private posts grew as Germanic towns established their own postal communications. Butchers' posts were also brought back into use.

In 1806, as a consequence of his defeat at the Battle of Slavkov, the Austrian Emperor had to renounce his title of Holy Roman Emperor. Consequently the Thurn-Taxis family — they were granted the title Counts of Thurn and Taxis in 1650 by the Emperor Ferdinand III — lost their hereditary Imperial Postal Patent General (*Reichspostgeneralpatent*). In later years, the counts of Thurn and Taxis signed agreements with the rulers of individual German states, which enabled

Franz von Taxis, the founder of the Taxis Post.

them to continue their postal communications.

At first, many German states entrusted the operation of postal communications to this mighty aristocratic family, perhaps because they were worried by the costs of setting up an alternative service, or doubted their own profitability. However, when the then German states realized that

Thurn-Taxis post office sign.

A mounted courier from the 17th century.

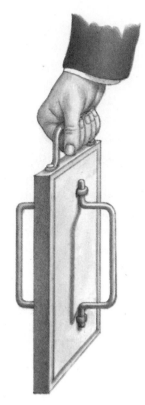

A letter collector of the Vienna Little Post, called *Klapperpost*. Each collector had a number, and announced his arrival with a rattle. The Little Post operated in Vienna in the last quarter of the 18th century, and at the beginning of the 19th century. Similar services were established in Prague.

A rattle belonging to a Vienna Little Post collector.

postal communications provided huge profits, changes soon followed. For example, Bavaria took over the Taxis post and paid the annual rent of 100,000 gold *tolars* between the years 1808 and 1815; the Taxis post operated in the state of Württemberg until 1851, when it was bought out and operated by the state itself.

The Taxis post was abolished in Germany in 1867, when Prussia bought out the Thurn-Taxis family rights to operate postal services for the sum of three million golden *tolars*, plus the right to have their future family correspondence carried free of charge.

Problems and Complaints

Even though they began to provide a wider public service, the spread of postal communications was hindered by high transport costs. While the cost of the postal service was originally met by the recipient, this principle was not implemented in all countries, and it was also subject to frequent changes. In 19th-century Austria, the sender would pay half the charge, and the recipient the other half. However, there were times when the cost had to be paid in full, either when

A postal coach standing in front of a village pub.

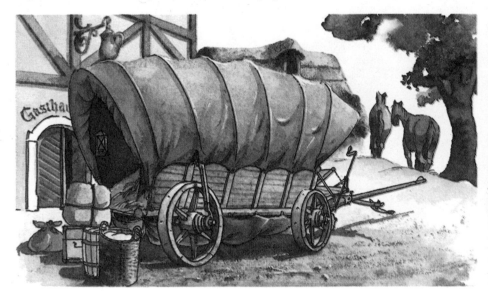

sending post or when it was being delivered.

It was also difficult to calculate the cost of posting a letter abroad, especially in central Europe, which at that time was divided into a great number of kingdoms, duchies, principalities, cantons, and free towns. While these would sign agreements concerning postal communications, each of them would have different postal regulations and rates. The postal charge would depend on the weight of mail, the distance between the sender and the recipient, and, finally, on the particular borders that might have to be crossed.

It is little wonder that complaints regarding excessive postal charges and the slow delivery of mail were frequent, often resulting in a boycott of the official post, which then suffered financial losses. For example, it was customary in England for individual merchants or firms to write their messages on a single sheet of paper. The first recipient would then cut out the relevant message and forward the remainder of the letter on to the next person. The postal cost was calculated per single sheet of paper. It was therefore necessary to pay for each individual sheet inserted in an envelope. The envelope also carried a charge, and this was perhaps why the use of envelopes was not common and spread very slowly.

Another problem was that coachmen frequently operated illegal postal services in heavily populated and industrial regions of England. Indeed, at times this was their principal occupation; the then postmaster of Manchester suggested that only about

half of the correspondence exchanged between Manchester and Liverpool was transported by the official post.

Improvements

These shortcomings in the postal service meant that reforms were necessary, including a simplified system of payment for mailed letters. Several attempts were made to introduce pre-paid letters, that is, letters for which postal costs were paid by the sender; in general they were unsuccessful. For example, Renouard de Villayer, who leased the Paris municipal post between 1653 and 1660, introduced a single postage that was paid in advance. The so-called *billet de port payé*, a certificate of pre-paid postage, was affixed to a letter before it was put into a postbox; this can be considered the predecessor of the postage stamp. It was even possible to affix a pre-paid reply form to the letter.

It was Henry Bishop, postmaster general of the English post between 1660 and 1663, who invented the postal stamp. While prior to this time the Italian courier services had used a form of hand-stamp to imprint a colourless postmark, Henry Bishop introduced postal stamps that imprinted the day and the month of posting in black, which helped, among other things, to monitor any complaints concerning negligence or lengthy delivery of mail. It would be a mistake, however, to view Bishop's postal stamps as being just like modern-day stamps for he actually required separate date-stamps for each day of the year. Several years later, the royal post modernized

A French stamp with the coat-of-arms of Renouard de Villayer, the founder of the Parisian Little Post.

Postage stamps of the London Penny Post. The letter 'W' denotes the office at Westminster, the letter 'L' denotes a City office in Lyme Street, the letter 'T' stands for Temple, and the letter 'P' stands for the City office at St Paul's.

Date stamps of the Penny Post. 'Mor: 8' denotes the morning of the 8th (day), and 'Af: 4' denotes the afternoon of the 4th (day).

these postal stamps by having the stamp divided into two halves. This decreased the number of stamps needed, because one half marked the respective month, while the other half imprinted the day of that month.

Further improvements followed when Robert Murray established the first London municipal post in 1680, managed by one William Dockwra. This post carried letters and parcels weighing up to one pound (which at that time equalled 454 grams)

throughout London for the very inexpensive rate of one penny. For this reason it was called the 'penny post'. For two pence, mail was delivered within a seventeen kilometre perimeter throughout the suburbs of London. The penny post had seven post offices and 400 collection boxes. Letters were delivered ten or twelve times a day in the centre of London, and four or five times in the suburbs.

In addition to these low postal charges, William Dockwra introduced two other innovations. Firstly, he made changes to Bishop's handstamps by having his heart-shaped stamps bear both the hour of posting, and the abbreviations 'Mor.' (morning), or 'Af.' (afternoon). Secondly, W. Dockwra introduced a triangular handstamp with the inscription PAID, to show that the sender had already paid the postage. In the middle of the stamp was a letter specifying one of the seven London post offices, for example, 'L' for Lyme Street, or 'W' for Westminster. This showed which post office was responsible for the delivery after the post had been collected from a post-box. As well, the abbreviation of the respective day of the week — such as MON, 'Monday' — was given under the post office letter. The penny post soon became a serious rival to the royal post, and it was therefore taken over by the state towards the end of 1682. Its handstamps, however, remained in use for some time afterwards.

Between the years 1819 and 1836 a unique postal system was adopted in the Kingdom of Sardinia. In order to send a letter, it was necessary to use a special paper with a stamp, which was imprinted in blue (and later in colour-free relief). The stamp depicted a naked boy riding a horse while blowing a horn, and the value of the stamp was given under the picture: fifteen *centesimi* for a letter dispatched to a distance of twenty-five kilometres; twenty-five *centesimi* for fifty-seven kilometres; or fifty *centesimi* over fifty-seven kilometres. These stamps were called *cavallini*, or 'the Sardinian horses', after the engraved picture. These letter papers, however, cannot be

Above:
Cavallini —
'the Sardinian Horses'.

Left:
An announcement
of the establishment
of the London
Penny Post.

James Chalmers, one of Rowland Hill's predecessors.

Rowland Hill, the proposer of a successful postal reform.

considered the predecessors of modern envelopes with an imprinted stamp, postal stationery, because the postage had to be paid separately.

All of the changes mentioned above were possible because at that time letters were confined principally to one area, or to one country. No matter what system of collecting postal charges was adopted in the individual countries, it was invariably expensive and inconvenient for the public. It is little wonder then that various proposals were made to simplify the collection of post, and to lower postal charges.

Rowland Hill's Postal Reform

Several attempts were made to introduce postage stamps. In 1823, Curry Gabriel Treffenberg, a Swedish army officer and consular official, proposed a postal reform which had twenty-three clauses, including a proposal to introduce postal envelopes with an imprinted stamp. The proposal was rejected because of its complicated structure, and Sweden did not introduce the first postage stamps until 1855.

Charles Knight, the London publisher, in 1834 suggested the introduction of a postal wrapper with an imprinted one-penny stamp, which hopefully would speed up the delivery of newspapers. In the same year, James Chalmers of Dundee developed Knight's idea further by suggesting the use of adhesive postal papers; he even printed some samples. In 1835, Lovrenc Košir, an official of civil administration in the Austrian province of Illyria and Lombardy, proposed to the Imperial Chamber in Vienna a way to simplify the postal system by introducing postage stamps. Košir's proposal was rejected as being too complicated.

The postal reforms that were proposed at this time were the result of external factors, namely that the huge growth in industrial development and in trade could not be served by the existing postal services; the postal service simply had to catch up.

Rowland Hill (1795–1879), first a country teacher and then postmaster general of Great Britain, suggested a postal reform whose implementation resulted in major changes to the postal systems of Britain and the rest of the world. Rowland Hill is today renowned as an outstanding postal reformer. Postage stamps bearing his portrait have been issued by a number of international postal administrations to commemorate important anniversaries of the first British postage stamps — which are also the world's first postage stamps.

In 1837 Hill submitted to the government a paper entitled 'Post Office Reform: Its Importance and Practicability'. Without trying to belittle Hill's achievement, it should be noted that there were not many original ideas in Hill's document: he sim-

The title page of Rowland Hill's paper on postal reform.

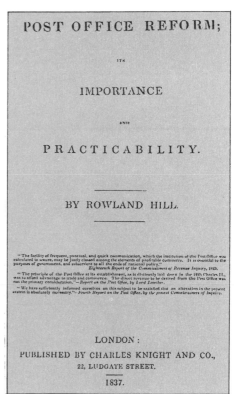

ply studied all previous postal reform proposals, and included the most appropriate ideas in his own paper.

The central point of Hill's reform was the introduction of a unified penny postage for all domestic mail weighing up to 15.5 grams, which replaced the former gradation of postal charges related to distance. The sender would pay the postage in advance, and the recipient would only pay for the delivered post if the postage had not been paid. Hill's document also briefly mentioned the idea of a label big enough to be stamped; this

Examples of the rejected first postage stamp designs.

would be affixed to the back of the letter as a sign of prepaid postage. Hill seems to have favoured postal stationery (envelopes with an imprinted stamp), and actively encouraged their introduction and use. The sale of envelopes and letter papers with the imprinted postage stamp designed by Charles Knight was highly recommended because it simplified postal payment. However, when Hill's plans concerning the postal reform were published, James Chalmers contacted the authorities and criticized Hill's proposals in great detail, stressing the advantage of his postage labels as compared to Hill's sheets of letter paper with their imprinted stamps.

Hill made a study of the French postal system, and concluded that the lowering of postal charges in Britain would lead to an increase in the amount of post sent, and thus would help to make the British post profitable.

At first the British postal administration considered his idea to be 'a wild fantasy', and it was not easy to have it accepted. However, a special parliamentary committee recommended the adoption of Rowland Hill's postal reform, with minor changes and additions, such as a recommendation to introduce adhesive postage stamps based on Chalmers' idea. Both Houses of Parliament then passed a Bill based on Hill's reform. The Act was submitted to Queen Victoria (1837–1901) for her royal assent, and the Act was signed on 17 August 1839. The approved postal reform took effect on 10 January 1840, when a new postal rate of one penny for an ordinary letter was also introduced.

A copy of Queen Victoria's portrait presented to the King of Portugal in 1840. It was painted by Alfred Edward Chalon, an English painter.

The conditions necessary for the further development of the British postal system were thus established.

The World's First Postage Stamps

Rowland Hill joined the civil service and was put in charge of implementing postal reform. He was assisted in this by a postage stamp competition that was organized by *The Times* in 1837. In Hill's view, it was important to design postage stamps with a special engraving that would be difficult, if not impossible, to forge. A competition was held to find the best design. Although hundreds of possible designs were submitted, neither Hill nor the jury were satisfied with the quality of the entries. For example, one entry consisted of an envelope-sized stamp depicting the Union Jack, with a central space for the address.

Several entrants suggested using the Queen's portrait, however it was the commemorative medal of Queen Victoria, issued in 1837 to mark her visit to the Guildhall, that became the model for the 'Penny Black'. The medal was designed by William Wyon. The Queen's portrait was copied from this and Charles and Frederick Heath became the engravers of Britain's — and the world's — first postage stamp.

The London firm Perkins, Bacon and Petch, who printed securities, was entrusted with issuing the stamps; they had to overcome a number of obstacles when preparing their issue. The 'Penny Black' was already on sale in London by 1 May 1840, although it only became valid on 6

William Wyon's commemorative medal of Queen Victoria.

May. As Rowland Hill noted in his diary, 'the post office was in great chaos on that day'. The stamp was issued in sheets of 240 (twenty horizontal rows of twelve stamps each) and a single sheet cost £1. At that time £1 equalled 20 shillings (*s.*), or 240 old pennies (*d.*). In order to prevent abuse or forgery, all stamps had corner letters, each stamp in the sheet having a different combination of letters. A similar device was used

with the blue 2*d.* stamp that appeared on sale several days later.

The world's first two adhesive postage stamps came into use on 6 May 1840. The 'Penny Black' and the two-penny stamp both depicted Queen Victoria, although the name of the stamp-issuing country was not given. Ever since this first issue tradition has been upheld, and British postage stamps always bear the portrait of the current sovereign.

The first postage stamps were printed using the technique of die-stamping from engraving, which was the most common printing technique at that time.

The world's first postage stamps.

A-A	A-B	A-C	A-D	A-E	A-F	A-G	A-H	A-I	A-J	A-K	A-L
B-A	B-B	B-C	B-D	B-E	B-F	B-G	B-H	B-I	B-J	B-K	B-L
C-A	C-B	C-C	C-D	C-E	C-F	C-G	C-H	C-I	C-J	C-K	C-L
D-A	D-B	D-C	D-D	D-E	D-F	D-G	D-H	D-I	D-J	D-K	D-L
E-A	E-B	E-C	E-D	E-E	E-F	E-G	E-H	E-I	E-J	E-K	E-L
F-A	F-B	F-C	F-D	F-E	F-F	F-G	F-H	F-I	F-J	F-K	F-L
G-A	G-B	G-C	G-D	G-E	G-F	G-G	G-H	G-I	G-J	G-K	G-L
H-A	H-B	H-C	H-D	H-E	H-F	H-G	H-H	H-I	H-J	H-K	H-L
I-A	I-B	I-C	I-D	I-E	I-F	I-G	I-H	I-I	I-J	I-K	I-L
J-A	J-B	J-C	J-D	J-E	J-F	J-G	J-H	J-I	J-J	J-K	J-L
K-A	K-B	K-C	K-D	K-E	K-F	K-G	K-H	K-I	K-J	K-K	K-L
L-A	L-B	L-C	L-D	L-E	L-F	L-G	L-H	L-I	L-J	L-K	L-L

A layout of corner letters on a sheet of the first English stamps. The twelve stamps in each horizontal row had the same letter in the left-hand corner: 'A' in the first row, 'B' in the second, 'C' in the third, and so on until the twentieth row, which bore the letter 'T'. Each stamp also had a letter in the right-hand corner, from the letter 'A' at the bottom to the letter 'L' at the top.

They were not perforated. The stamps were printed on handmade paper, and watermarked with small crown symbols. A watermark is a sign, such as a drawing, inscription, abbreviation, numeral, or ornament, which is included in the manufacture of paper, and is visible only when the paper is held against the light. Because it is created during the paper manufacturing process, it remains permanent and cannot be removed.

The postage stamps of the United Kingdom and Ireland show the same ageless portrait of Queen Victoria until 1900 because the Queen ordained that her portrait remain unchanged. Only some postage stamps issued in the late 1890s by the British colonies, such as Canada, Newfoundland, and New South Wales, depict Queen Victoria as an elderly woman in a widow's veil.

Because these adhesive postage stamps were a novelty for the public, the post office had the instructions on how to use them printed at the edge of every sheet of stamps. The text accompanying the stamp was as follows: 'Price 1*d* Per Label. 1ˢ/- Per Row of 12. £ 1 Per Sheet. Place the Label ABOVE the Address and towards the RIGHT HAND SIDE of letter. In Wetting the Back be careful not to remove the Cement'.

The Maltese Cross postage stamp, used to cancel the first English stamps.

Lovrenc Košir, the pioneer of the world's first postage stamp, depicted on an Austrian stamp.

The stamps affixed to letters to pay for their delivery were cancelled by a postmark. (A cancellation is any mark used on a stamp to prevent it being used or reused). This was the origin of the later classification of stamps into three categories: mint stamps, uncancelled used stamps, and used stamps. It is interesting to note that at that time the postage stamps officially were called 'labels'. The term 'postage stamps', or the abbreviated form 'stamp', only came to be used later.

For the first ten years of its use the lower postal rate in stamps resulted in huge losses for the British post office. However, the results foreseen by Hill finally were achieved. In consequence of simplifying the postal services, in 1864 the post carried 642 million letters in England alone, compared with the much smaller figure of 78 million letters in 1838.

Rowland Hill died on 27 August 1879 holding the office of postmaster general. He was buried in Westminster Abbey next to James Watt (1736–1819), the Scottish inventor of the steam-engine, which itself brought about revolutionary changes in industry, while the postage stamp unveiled new possibilities in the postal system. Hill's statue, which was unveiled in London in 1882, commemorates his pre-eminence in postal history. His major contribution was the introduction of postage stamps and the lowering and simplification of the postal rate. He was lucky to have lived in England, where the conditions for postal reform were more favourable than, for example, those facing Treffenberg in Sweden, or Košir in Austria.

Lovrenc Košir published a pamphlet in 1858 in which he defended his claim as the originator and designer of the world's first postage stamp. Feeling he had suffered a great injustice, Košir appealed to the First Congress of the Universal Postal Union, which was held in Bern in 1874. He even sent letters to all the countries of the world that had by then issued their own postage stamps, claiming to be the inventor of the first stamp, and indeed the originator of postal reform. Košir demanded that he should at the very least be refunded for the costs of working on his postal reform proposals. These letters, however, met with no response.

In Great Britain, postal stationery — envelopes and covers (any envelope, wrapper or other type cover) — were issued simultaneously with the first two postage stamps. The envelopes and covers were issued in two colours and two denominations, like the first stamps. The envelopes and covers bearing the inscription 'POSTAGE ONE PENNY' had a black-lined drawing, while the others, inscribed with 'POSTAGE TWO PENCE', had a blue-lined drawing. The postal stationery had a drawing that symbolized the British Empire on one side. Like the stamp, a competition had been held to design the stationery. The winner was William Mulready, a well-known graphic art-

The much-criticized Mulready's postal stationery.

ist and illustrator, who had been invited by the Exchequer to participate in the competition.

Although Rowland Hill considered postal stationery to be a very important component of his post office reform, things did not go according to plan. Several days after the first issue of this postal stationery — immediately nicknamed 'Mulreadys' — it was ridiculed in satirical poems and caricatures. Thus in January 1841 postal stationery was withdrawn from circulation, to be followed

by the withdrawal of the 2d. stationery in April of the same year. The decision was taken by the very Exchequer that had invited Mulready to take part in the competition in the first place.

Mulready's failure did not, however, discourage the later designers of postal stationery. The much-criticized 'Mulreadys' were in a sense rehabilitated when at a London philatelic exhibition in 1897 a blue label with a reproduction of Mulready's allegorical drawing was issued.

3 The Postage Stamp Continues to Develop

Postage Stamps Conquer the World

The importance of the postage stamp in the further improvement and development of postal systems was soon appreciated in other countries. Following England's example, the postal administrations of nearly all the independent countries of Europe and America, including their principal colonies, introduced postage stamps, although the development of issuing stamps in Asia and in parts of Africa was a lengthier process. At the turn of the century, postage stamps had become everyday objects, even in distant parts of the world.

The Swiss canton of Zürich was the second in the world to issue stamps. In 1843 it issued two stamps of four- and six-*rapp* denominations, which had a simple numerical design. In the same year, the Brazilian empire became, rather surprisingly, the third to issue stamps. Philatelists nicknamed the first edition of these stamps 'Bulls' Eyes', with the two following 'Goats' Eyes', and 'Cats' Eyes', respectively, because of their shapes. The Swiss canton of Geneva was the fourth to issue stamps, followed in 1845 by the canton of Basel, which issued a postage stamp with its

The first stamps from the Swiss canton of Zürich and their cancellations (top and bottom).

coat-of-arms above a dove, which became the symbol of postal services. This stamp, called the 'Basel Dove', soon became popular with collectors because it was the first postage stamp issued with several variations in colour.

In 1845 the first postage stamps in the United States appeared. They were not, however, issued by the United States postal administration, but by the post-

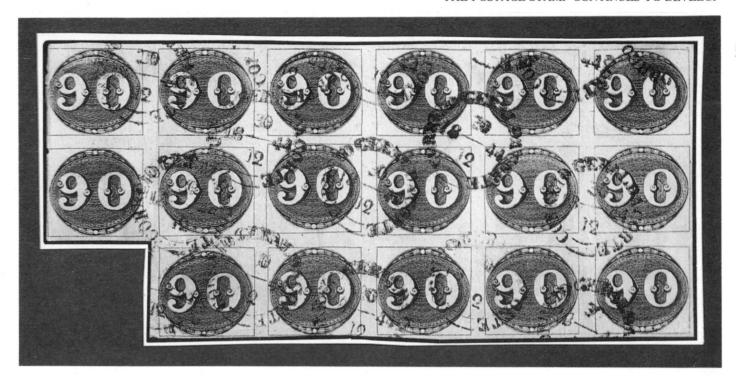

Above: An example of the Brazilian issue of 'Bulls' Eyes'.

Right: A five-*centime* stamp from the canton of Geneva, the postage due to deliver a letter within the city itself. The stamp bears an inscription 'PORT LOCAL', the local postage, on its lower edge. The postage for letters delivered throughout the canton required two five-*centime* stamps. Therefore, the two adjacent stamps in a sheet were linked at the top with the inscription, '10. PORT CANTONAL. CENT.', or, the regional postage of ten *centimes*. This represented a dual stamp to the value of five plus five *centimes*.

Right, below: The popular 'Basel Dove'.

masters in several towns, such as Alexandria (Virginia), Baltimore (Maryland), New York (City, New York), and St. Louis (Missouri), which decided to issue their own local stamps. The stamps are either simple postmarks showing certain denominations, or primitively printed emergency issues. The only exception is the New York stamp, which incorporates President Washington's 'bank-

Above: The most valuable Canadian stamp, one of the first stamps bearing the inscription 'CANADA'.

Above: A miniature sheet issued by the Italian Post Office to commemorate the world philatelic exhibition 'Italia 1985'. It consists of nine stamps, each depicting the stamp of one former Italian state: Parma, Naples, Sicily, Modena, the Holy See, Tuscany, Sardinia, Romagna, Austrian Lombardy, and Venice.

note portrayal'. These first American stamps today are called postmasters' stamps; they are rare, and considered to be of great value.

Later, when United States federal stamps were issued, these postmasters' stamps were invalidated. In 1861, when the Civil

Above right: A stamps issued in 1970 by the French Post Office to commemorate the 100th anniversary of an issue printed at Bordeaux during the Franco-Prussian War.

Right: The coach used by the French Post Office for transporting mail sent from England to India between Calais and Marseilles, based on an agreement signed in 1839 by France and Great Britain. This route was part of the postal links via the Mediterranean Sea, Egypt, and the Red Sea to the Indian Ocean. These postal links speeded up the movement of mail formerly transported round Africa. A British Post Office courier accompanied the mail.

An Austrian 'fast' coach, from the beginning of the 19th century.

War started, in order to prevent the smuggling of stamps from enemy-held territory, the earlier stamp issues lost their currency. It is a postal peculiarity of the United States that all stamps issued since the beginning of August 1861 are still valid.

Hill's postal reform did not go unnoticed in Canada, which at that time was a British colony. The Canadians, however, did not wait for instructions from the motherland on how to carry out postal reform. Instead, the governor general of British North America summoned his provincial officials to a meeting in Toronto, which resulted in the unification and lowering of the postal rate. In addition, governments of individual provinces became responsible for their own postal administrations. On 9 April 1851, the first three postage stamps marked CANADA were issued: the deep-red 'Beaver'; the 6*d.* slate-violet 'Prince Albert', and 12*d.*

A milestone in Saxony (Germany). These milestones were erected at the beginning of the 18th century on the order of King Friedrich August I (1694–1773). They indicated both direction and distance, thus improving transport.

An American coach, which carried passengers in the second half of the 19th century.

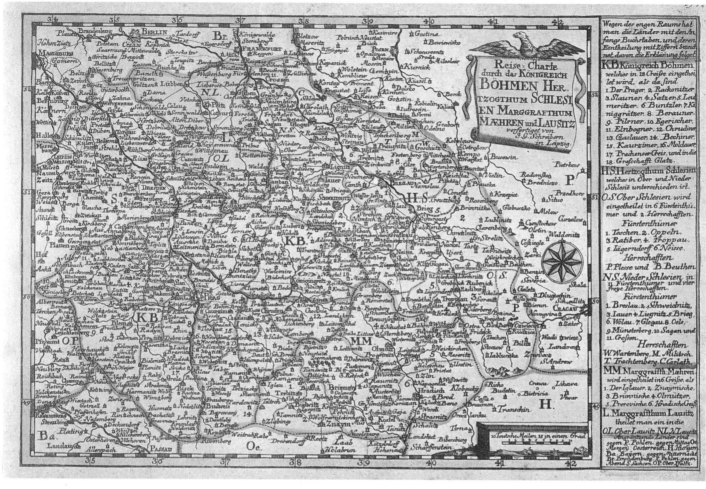

Above: A travel map of Bohemia, Moravia and Silesia from the mid-19th century.

Right: The Parliament Hall in Bern where the first International Congress met.

Below: Heinrich von Stephan (1831—1897), the German postmaster general.

'Queen Victoria'. In mint condition, these stamps are the most valuable of all Canadian stamps.

In the first half of the 19th century, postmaster generals and post office administrators in individual countries realized that their individual system could not competently sustain postal links abroad. They understood that it would be wrong to continue operating their own postal links to remote countries, while permitting foreign postal links on their own territory. There thus appeared attempts by the postal administrations of various countries to establish mutually convenient links, with England, France, Russia, Prussia, and Austria signing a number of bilateral postal agreements on postal rates, currency, weight units, and transit facilities through other countries. While these agreements reflected the split character of the world's postal system, they nevertheless resulted in certain advances and valuable experience.

Dozens of transit facilities were agreed and concluded by the countries, permitting the passage of letters across the world; it was,

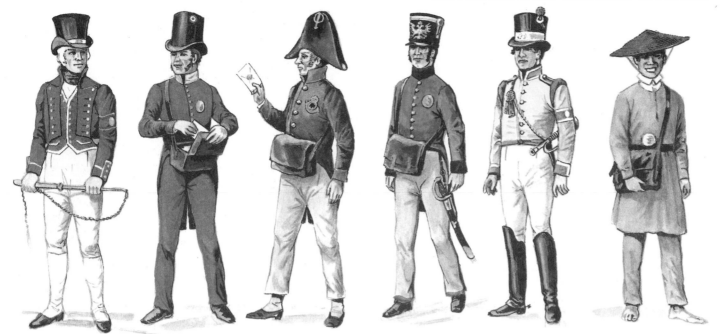

Above, from left to right: Post office couriers and postilions (19th century) — a Swedish courier, a French postilion, a Prussian postilion, a Russian postilion, a Saxonian postilion, a Surabayan courier.

a

b

d

c

e

however, more difficult to specify the route of each letter and to calculate its correct postage. The individual agreements also took account of local customs, and used preferential treatment in relation to some countries. American trade and industry found it very difficult to accept that, for example, European mail dispatched to a particular destination in the

Examples of postboxes from the 19th century: a) Great Britain (1853), b) Austria (*c.* 1850), c) Hesse (*c.* 1865), d) Germany (1896), and e) Germany (*c.* 1900).

The *Savannah*, an American postal frigate which crossed the Atlantic in 1819. Although a sailing vessel, it was also equipped with a steam engine.

An 1829 steam-engine coach built by the Englishman William Henry James. The boiler and steam engine were protected against shaking by leaf springs.

The first Swedish postal bus from 1923, which was specially adapted for driving in wintery conditions.

United States would have a different postage value according to which route it had travelled and through how many countries.

Montgomery Blair, at that time postmaster general of the United States, suggested that an international conference be held in Paris to discuss the main principles of a postal communications agreement. The conference took place in 1863, but it did not reach any concrete agreements. All of its participants, however, did agree that bilateral postal agreements could not guarantee any further improvements in international postal communications.

A solution was achieved at the 1874 Bern International Postal Congress, which was initiated by Heinrich von Stephan, the German postmaster general. Representatives of the twenty-two participating countries signed an International Postal Agreement, and established the General Postal Union (*Union Général des Postes*). This agreement, written in French, established a fifteen-gram letter as the basis for all calculations, and stipulated the postal charge of twenty-five *centimes* for it. It was further agreed that the collected postal fees would be retained by the collecting postal administration, thereby removing the need to arrange mutual reimbursements. It was also decided that the transit of mail throughout foreign territory would be permitted upon the payment of a fee, whose amount was calculated according to weight of the item.

The Agreement was signed by all the participating delegations, except France, who added her signature in 1875. Australia did not take part in the 1874 Congress, and thus does not belong among the founding-member states of General Postal Union.

The Second Congress, which took place four years later in Paris, renamed the organization the Universal Postal Union (*Union Postale Universalle,* or UPU). Its membership increased rapidly, and by 1900 it had over sixty members. Today the UPU has

Right: The present-day seat of the Universal Postal Union in Bern.

Three international reply coupons: a) Roman type, b) London type, c) Viennese type. They are issued by the member states of the UPU in accordance with the decision of the 1906 International Postal Congress. The sender encloses with his letter a prepaid reply coupon stamped by the issuing post office. The addressee in any member country of the UPU can exchange this coupon at a post office to pay the postage on a letter with his reply. In addition to international reply coupons, some post offices use the so-called 'regional reply coupons' on their own territories. One example is d) L'union Française reply coupons, which are valid between France and her overseas territories Monaco and Andorra.

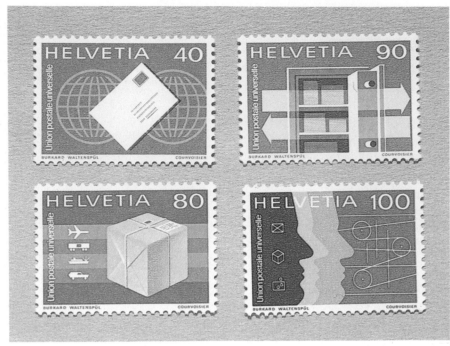

Above: **Stamps issued for the International Office of the UPU in 1975.**

An Australian stamp overprinted with 'SPECIMEN', and a German stamp overprinted with 'MUSTER'.

over 160 members. The main aims of the UPU are to establish a single postal territory of all its member states in order to permit a mutual exchange of post; to simplify and promote international postal communications; to develop single postal rates internationally; to promote the exchange of information concerning the organization of postal systems; and to participate in providing technical assistance for the member states.

Examples of postboxes from the 20th century: a) Great Britain, b) Austria, c) France, d) Czechoslovakia

The highest organ of the UPU is its Congress, which usually meets every five years. It reviews the World Postal Agreement and other conventions if initiated to do so by any of its member states. For example, the 1878 Paris Congress established basic postal rates for registered letters and postal orders; the 1880 Paris Conference fixed postal rates for the delivery of parcels; the 1891 Vienna Congress agreed rates for newspaper delivery by post.

French is the official working language of the UPU, and its international office is situated in Bern. Each member state pledges to send examples of all its postal stationery to other member states through the UPU so that each country has a knowledge of all stamps issued by other UPU members. Many countries over-

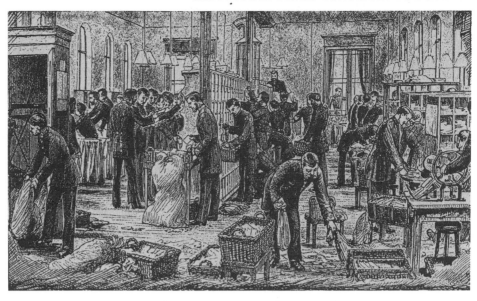

Sorting mail according to destination at a Berlin post office *c.* 1900.

print these stamps as SPECIMEN, MUSTER, MUESTRA, PROVA, SAGGIO, and so on. Since 1957 the Swiss Post Office has been issuing postage stamps with the inscription UNION POSTALE UNIVERSELLE and HELVETIA for the International Office of the UPU. Their denominations are in Swiss currency. In 1947 the Universal Postal Union became an associate specialized member of the United Nations.

Part of an automatic letter-sorting machine.

a

b

Examples of meter stamps (*from top to bottom*): a) meter stamps used to frank mail at post office counters (Great Britain, Belgium, Liechtenstein, Japan, Burma); b) meter labels used by companies and firms, which send huge amounts of mail, to pay the postage. They are accompanied by the firm's name or its logo, an inscription or an illustration (Germany, France, Canada, US, Czechoslovakia).

Above, from top to bottom:
Meter postage stamps — Switzerland, Austria, Belgium, Germany.

Postal Services of Today and Tomorrow

The efficiency of the present-day post is enormous. Over half a million postal offices operate in the world; they deliver 160 billion letters and postcards, and over two billion parcels every year. In many countries postal administrations use modern technology to facilitate their work, such as semi-automatic letter-sorting machines and cancelling machines. In order to make sorting easier, postage stamps today are printed on paper with fluorescent or phosphorescent traces, or they have a luminous overprint in the form of dots, ribbons, or interrupted lines. At times, the barcodes are printed on stamps etc. during semi-automatic sorting.

The introduction of postal codes, placed before or after the place name, facilitate the full use of automation. Some postal administrations have selected a postal code formed from the letters of the alphabet; others have chosen a numerical code. However, some countries, such as Great Britain and France, prefer the mixed postal code, combining letters and numerals. So far, there is no international agreement on postal codes.

The use of metering machines has spread quickly. While in some countries they had already been introduced before the Second World War, at present nearly half the post is delivered without using postage stamps. Instead, the post carries meter postage stamps; even these meter stamps are not without interest and value for some philatelists.

In 1976, the Swiss post office introduced slot machines that dispensed meter stamps. The slot machines work like metering ma-

Below: A satellite ground station, used to transmit messages, is depicted on a block of four Belgian stamps issued in 1971. They commemorate the third day of l'Union Internationale des Telecommunications.

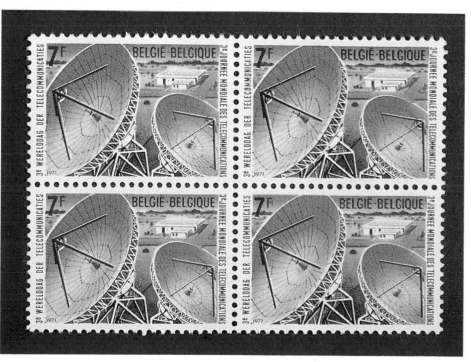

The American telecommunications satellite 'Intelsat III' depicted on a Malaysian stamp, and the Soviet 'Molniya' depicted on a Czechoslovak Stamp.

chines: when the required postal denomination is selected, ranging from 00.05 to 99.95 Swiss francs, and the appropriate coins are inserted, the machine issues an unperforated label, 40×32 mm. The value of the label is in red on a blue and grey background. Later, similar slot-metering machines were introduced in other countries, such as Germany, France, Great Britain, Austria, and Finland.

Another kind of modern postal communication involves the use of satellites, which enable black-and-white graphics, drawings, and diagrams, and texts to be sent over long distances in a matter of minutes.

For example, if it is Tuesday 5.30 pm in Toronto, a document will reach London seconds later, and, only because it is 10.30 pm in London, will it be delivered on Wednesday morning; the reply, if sent immediately, can then reach Toronto on the same day, five hours earlier.

4 *Philately and Philatelists*

The Origins of Philately

The first postage stamps issued in England in 1840 received great interest from stamp collectors and others. It is recorded in newspaper advertisements of the time that some people even used cancelled stamps to paper the walls in their homes!

It cannot be said with certainty who was the first true collector of postage stamps, however, Dr John Edward Gray (1800–1875), who worked in the British Museum, is considered to be one of the pioneers of philately. Gray began collecting postage stamps soon after they appeared, and also prepared a catalogue of stamps that was reprinted six times.

It was a certain M. Herpin, probably a pseudonym, who named this new form of collecting. On 15 November 1864 he published an article entitled *Baptême* ('Baptism') in a magazine called *Le Collectionneur de Timbres-Poste*. M. Herpin suggested the use of two terms 'philately' and 'philatelist', for the activity and collector of stamps. The terms are derived from the Greek *phileo*, 'I love', and *ateleia*, 'free from charges', in the sense that postage stamps replaced a cash postal charge. However, these words can also be interpreted as derived from the Greek word *philos*, 'friend', and *ateleia*.

Other names for this new collecting activity were suggested, such as timbrophilia and timbrology, the science of postage stamps, but these were not generally adopted. The word 'timbrology' only has been preserved in the name of a French magazine, *L' Echo de la Timbrologie*, and it is occasionally used in French. The word 'timbrophilia', the love of stamps, which is de-

Dr John Edward Gray's stamp catalogue of 1862.

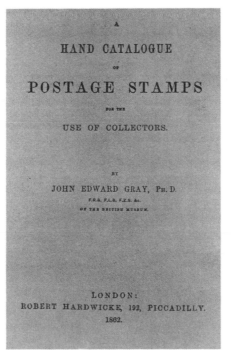

rived from the word *timbrophil*, a lover of stamps, has been preserved in the title, *'L' Union des Timbrophiles de Luxembourg'*, The Luxembourg Union of Friends of Postage Stamps, which was founded in 1890.

Although the first newspaper and magazine articles on postage stamps had already appeared by 1840, philatelists had to wait until the 1860s for the first specialized philatelic magazines. Most of these were short-lived, and only appeared for several issues.

At first the pioneers of philately collected postage stamps from around the world, and were only just beginning to learn the delights of stamp collecting. They compiled their collections without the assistance of any catalogues, manuals, or previous knowledge; they could not have realized they were preparing the way for a great collecting activity that eventually would spread world-wide.

Dealers also soon focused their attention on philately. They quickly realized that used, or cancelled, postage stamps might become collectors' items, and that it might be possible to sell them on to collectors who had not been fortunate enough to possess certain stamps, or had not been able to exchange them for some stamps of their own.

The beginnings of philately, however, were not without problems. For example, in a newspaper article of 1863, the French post's director general wrote expressing his great amazement that, for reasons difficult to understand, some people had parcels of cancelled postage stamps sent to them (it seems that he was not too worried about the breach of postal secrecy). A year later the director general returned to the same topic, but this time he was more specific, writing that until the true reason was established for this activity, searching out and collecting used postage stamps seemed to have suspicious, if not illegal, motives. Similar views became rather persistent: in 1875 the French minister of post and telegraph services authorized an investigation into

Measuring the perforations of a postage stamp on a perforation gauge.

Examples of philatelic magazines from the 19th century: *Die Post* (German), *Le Timbre Post* (Belgian), *The Stamp Collector's Magazine* (English),

'several dealers who dared to trade cancelled postage stamps in the very centre of Paris'.

Dealing in postage stamps created pre-conditions for the systematic and specialized collecting of stamps, and thus positively influenced the development of philately. Dealers began to issue the first postage stamp catalogues, albums, magazines, and specialized literature. This in turn encouraged collectors to take up more serious studies, and the thorough investigation of stamps. Collectors gradually moved from hoarding stamps to the study of the history and technical details of stamp production, for example, extraordinary though it may seem, in 1866 the Frenchman Jacques Amable

Legrand (1820—1912) discovered a way of measuring the perforation of postage stamps. He designed a perforation gauge, so familiar to philatelists nowadays, and a year later published a manual on watermarks.

The First Philatelic Societies and Exhibitions

In the 1860s philatelists established their first societies in France, Canada, England, Germany, and Belgium. (For our purposes, earlier collectors' associations, who were only marginally interested in postage stamps, can be disregarded.)

These first philatelic societies, like the first philatelic magazines, were short-lived affairs, although there were some exceptions, such as The Philatelic Society, established in London in 1869 and renamed The Royal Philatelic Society in 1906. As such it exists to the present day.

The first postage stamp exhibitions were held simultaneously with the founding of the first philatelic societies. The aim of these exhibitions was primarily to publicize philately, although initially only a few philatelists exhibited their collections. It is not possible today to ascertain the detailed history of the philatelic exhibitions, however the 1852 Philatelic Exhibition in Brussels is considered to be the first postage stamp exhibition. In Germany, the first stamp exhibition took place in Dresden in 1870, and Alfred Moschkau (1840–1912) was the sole exhibitor. Moschkau was by far the most versatile German philatelist of his day, with his outstandingly thorough knowledge of postage stamps.

This brief survey shows that the origins of philately can definitely be dated from the 1860s. While philately as a hobby grew quickly, it should be kept in mind that it was only relatively wealthy people who could devote their time to it and who joined philatelic societies.

Philately has attracted millions of followers since the 1860s, and a number of particular fields of interest have developed. Present-day philatelists are interested

An example of commemorative miniature sheets: Great Britain.

Postage stamps which do not bear the name of the stamp-issuing country (*from left to right*): Bosnia-Herzegovina; Great Britain; Tsarist Russia; Turkey; a stamp issued by the Northern German Postal Society for post offices in Alsace-Lorraine and in Prussian-occupied French territory (1870—1871); and the German Reich.

chiefly in traditional philately, aerophilately, thematic philately, postal history, and collecting postal stationery.

The Introduction of the Postage Stamp

There is probably no one in the world who does not know what a postage stamp looks like. In any case, it is worth stating that officially a stamp is postal stationery issued by an authorized body, usually a government, for the pre-payment of the delivery of post, or to meet various postal charges. A stamp therefore differs from a postal label, which cannot fulfil these functions.

If we look at a stamp carefully, we can see on its face a picture or decorative illustrations, the name of the country issuing the stamp, and its nominal — or postage — value. The value is usually given in Arabic numerals but does not specify the currency. In addition to this basic information, there might be an additional inscription that describes the picture on the stamp, for example MARCO POLO (1254—1954), or its purpose, for example DIENSTMARKE ('official stamp'); or it might state the

History tells us about many important rulers who could not write. The French King Charlemagne (AD 784—814) was one of these. His 'signature' is given on a document sealed at Kufstein on 31 August AD 790. The lozenge motif and a cross were executed by the king himself, whereas the monogram letters and other words (*Signum + Caroli Gloriosissimi Regis* — the Sign of Charles the Greatest King) were written by a scribe.

reason for a stamp issue, and its date, for example COMMONWEALTH GAMES, EDINBURGH 1966. The inscription tends to be as short as possible, although it is slightly longer on a miniature sheet, that is, postal stationery specially printed for information purposes, such as, LONDON 1980 INTERNATIONAL STAMP EXHIBITION BRITISH POST OFFICE FIRST MINIATURE SHEET.

Some stamps bear only additional inscriptions, or no inscriptions at all. The basic inscription — the name of the stamp-issuing country — is not given on British stamps, which bear the portrait of the current sovereign, or on the tsarist Russian stamps, or on some early stamps from Austria, Bosnia and Hercegovina (former Yugoslavia), which bear particu-

lar coats-of-arms or the current ruler's portrait.

Some Turkish stamps from the Sultanate period depict the Great Seal. Called *tughra*, which is often the main motif on these Turkish stamps, the Great Seal is of interesting origin. Because the Turkish Sultan Murad I, who ruled between 1359 and 1389, could not write, he put his fingerprints on a document as a mark of his approval. In 1365 one of his 'imprints' was stylized, and used to make the Great Seal, which became symbolic of state power. The picture of the *tughra* also appeared on Saudi-Arabian stamps between 1934 and 1945.

Occasionally the name of the stamp-issuing country is not given for political reasons, as for

Stamps with inscriptions in two languages (Canada, Belgium), and three languages (Switzerland).

A 1918 American stamp with an inverted centre.

A 1951 Chinese stamp. The numbers on the bottom edge of the stamp signify the twelfth issue of a series of four stamps; the fourth stamp in this series, the sixty-eighth stamp since the beginning of the issue.

example on the stamps issued in 1870 by the Northern German Postal Society for use on Prussian-occupied French territory. The name of the stamp-issuing country is not usually given on postage-due stamps, official stamps, and newspaper stamps because they are used for domestic postal communications only.

The inscription on a stamp is nearly always given in the official language of the issuing state. However, as the UPU stipulates that the name of the stamp-issuing country has to be given in Roman characters, there are some countries that have to use dual inscriptions, in the language of the country, and in Roman characters. If there are two official languages in a country, the inscriptions are given in both languages, as for example on Canadian stamps since 1927, where English CANADA POST, and French CANADA POSTES are both used; Belgian stamps have inscriptions in French BELGIQUE and Flemish BEL-

Right, clockwise from left to right: **Great Britain, Denmark, France, the Soviet Union (former), Spain, Norway, Germany (former), Sweden.**

53

Examples of commemorative stamps: Great Britain, Liechtenstein, Austria, Finland, US, and Nauru.

GIE; South African stamps have inscriptions in English SOUTH AFRICA, and Afrikaans SUID-AFRIKA. The Postal Administration of the United Nations issues some stamps on which the issuer's name is given in five out of its six official languages (not in Arabic), for example in Chinese, English, French, Russian, and Spanish. Their order changes regularly. There are other reasons for using the language other than the official one. For example, Latin on Swiss stamps HELVETIA, CONFEDERATIO HELVETICA replaces the three official languages, which are German, French, and Italian. The UN stamps issued in Vienna are always printed in German.

A stamp illustration is not usually in a frame, although some exceptions have appeared in recent years. The frame might just be a line, or the central part of a stamp might be framed decoratively. In such cases, stamps with the centre inverted can be issued; one example is the twenty-four-cent airmail stamp issued by the United States in 1918.

The face side of a stamp often bears the name of a designer and an engraver, the year of issue, (serial number stamps issued by the Chinese People's Republic give the number of the issue, the number of stamps in the issue, and the stamp's serial number), the publisher, and so on. One of the two Latin abbreviations 'DEL' (from *delineavit,* drawn by), or 'PINX' (from *pinxit,* traced by) is put before or after the designer's name, while the abbreviation 'SC.' (from *sculpsit,* engraved by) stands beside the engraver's name. The edge is created by the line where the stamp was separated by a cut, perforation, puncture, or a cut-out.

On the back of an unused stamp there may be control numerals, various signs, or even some text printed. This is done for statistical purposes, and for security reasons. The back of the stamp is impregnated with glue. In some countries, however, such as North Vietnam, postal administrations issue stamps without glue in order to prevent them from sticking together; it is therefore necessary to use glue to affix such a stamp. The glue used with some early issues — for example, Austrian stamps from the end of the 19th century — was so effective that removing these stamps from the surface they are stuck to is very difficult. The glue used on other stamps, however, was not so efficient. For example, the Württemberg royal post had difficulties with its very first stamp issue in 1851 because the stamps would not adhere to the envelope properly. A certain solution was thus necessary. Sugar-beet, grown widely in the Württemberg region, was added to the postal glue; the glue did improve, but it was rather sweet. The royal post issued a warning that the back of a stamp was to be wetted only slightly before affixing it on to an envelope.

Today, water-soluble glue is used on stamps. Some countries, such as Sierra Leone and the United States, have issued self-adhering postage stamps, which have their glue protected by a special paper or foil that is removed before the stamp is affixed. In the past glue was applied manually, but nowadays it is put on by machines. Postage stamps are now printed on paper that has already been impregnated with glue.

Varieties of Postage Stamps

The first stamps were issued to cover postal charges for carrying other mail, and providing other postal services. Stamps that have been created with various designations and for various purposes have been issued since their invention. Some were issued in all the countries of the world, while others were used only for short periods of time, and were issued by a small number of postal administrations.

Definitive stamps were commonplace in the past as they are today. They are often smaller in size, and are issued in large numbers of up to several hundred millions. Their principal function is to cover postal charges. Definitive stamps do not usually appear as a single stamp issue, but are printed in series of two or more stamps with different nominal values; sometimes the same illustration in different colours is used. The term 'issue' is used, in addition to the term 'series', to refer to a stamp or several stamps that are put into circulation simultaneously.

Commemorative stamps are issued by all countries in the world. In addition to their main function of covering postal charges, they have a publicity value. Commemorative stamps are issued to mark important public anniversaries and events, or to celebrate art, natural scenery, sport, and so on. The number of commemorative stamps in one issue is generally not too great, but there have been some exceptions, such as the two-cent stamp issued by the United States in 1932 to commemorate the 200th Anniversary of George Washington's birth. This issue numbered 4,222,198,300.

Charity stamps are a special category of commemorative stamps. Their nominal value consists of their definitive value plus a surcharge, which is intended for non-postal purposes, that is, to support some kind of charitable cause.

Clockwise, from left to right: **Examples of charity stamps: from Argentina, Luxembourg, Austria, Belgium, Yugoslavia, Switzerland and France.**

Above, clockwise from left to right: Examples of airmail stamps — Czechoslovakia, the German Reich, US, the Soviet Union (former), Italy, Columbia and Australia.

Examples of newspaper stamps: Czechoslovakia (*left and centre*), Austria (*right*).

There is a long tradition of these stamps, with a surcharge which benefits charities such as the Red Cross (France) or children (Switzerland).

Some stamps are issued specifically for certain kinds of postal carriage. Airmail stamps are the most common in this category. They appeared for the first time in 1917 in Italy, and with the gradual development of air transport after the First World War, other countries began to issue airmail stamps. The airmail surcharge for carrying post within individual countries and continents was abolished after the Second World War; airmail stamps ceased to be important, but some countries, such as the United States, still issue airmail stamps to carry post overseas.

In the mid-19th century, Austria was the first country in the world to issue newspaper stamps, by which newspapers could be delivered at a lower charge. Within several years these newspaper stamps were introduced in other countries, such as France and the United States. They are no longer in use.

Official stamps, express delivery stamps, personal delivery stamps, and parcel stamps are further categories which can also be collected.

Postage-due stamps differ from the stamps mentioned above because they are used only by the post office. The public come across these particular stamps only if a letter has been posted without any postage at all, or if the stamp or stamps affixed to the postal item have lower denominations than required.

The Recalling of Stamps

Postage stamps that have already been distributed can occasionally be recalled to the printers. In such cases the stamps are overprinted by altering their face value, their type, or the name of the stamp-issuing country, as well as commemorating national or international events.

Postal administrations will usually recall a stamp if a new issue has to be put into circulation fast, or if there are large quantities of stamp stocks remaining. In philatelic terminology this is called either an 'overprint', or a 'surcharge'.

A surcharge, which alters the face value of a stamp, is used when postal rates are changed, fiscal reforms are introduced, or if there is a shortage of certain denominations.

In the last century, postal administrations in some countries provided postage stamps for their own colonies and other countries by overprinting their own domestic stamps. For instance, some British stamps bear the overprint CYPRUS; some French stamps are overprinted with ALEXANDRIA; and some German stamps with CHINA. During the First World War, German stamps were overprinted with BELGIEN, and the denomination in Belgian currency, such as three *centimes*. These stamps were used in German-occupied Belgian territory.

An example of altering type is the Czechoslovak 1922 definitive stamp, which was transformed

Examples of express delivery stamps: Costa Rica, Canada, Czechoslovakia, US.

later into a postage-due stamp.

Postcards, a cardboard paper with an impressed stamp, or envelopes can also be altered with an overprint. France issued envelopes for its pneumatic post in 1887, reducing the value of impressed stamps from seventy-five to sixty *centimes* by the overprint TAXE RÉDUITE 60 C. The 1902 Edward VII English postcard, franked with $^{1}/_{2}$ *d.* was overprinted with the text ADMIRALTY OFFICIAL a year later, and became the official Admiralty Board postcard.

When talking about overprints and surcharges, it is important to mention the so-called pre-cancels, which are stamps that are already invalidated by a special postmark. They are designated to cover postal charges on mail posted in bulk, so that the post

Examples of official stamps (*below*): Pakistan, Luxembourg, Bavaria, Costa Rica, Czechoslovakia, East Germany (*former*), Bulgaria.

Examples of parcel stamps (*bottom*): US, Bulgaria, Belgium, France, Italy.

office does not have to cancel these stamps daily. They are used in France, Belgium, Canada, and the United States. Since 1953 France has been issuing pre-cancels that incorporate the cancelling postmark as part of the stamp's design. The United States issued its first pre-cancel in 1974.

Stamp Shapes and Sizes

In addition to the common rectangular and square ones, stamps come in various shapes. They might be triangular, such as the 1898 Turkish issues, or quadrilateral, as in the 1973 Portuguese Guinea stamps.

At first, an unusual stamp shape was used to distinguish special-purpose stamps from ordinary stamps. Examples are the triangular Austrian express delivery stamps; triangular Czechoslovak recorded delivery stamps; or hexagonal Belgian telegraph stamps. At present, unusual stamp shapes are used to encourage interest among stamp collectors.

A particular Iraqi stamp is a good example, being a perforated square stamp with the design enclosed by a perforated circle; if the sides of the stamp are separated, a perforated circular stamp is the result.

The Jordanian Post Office issued unperforated circular stamps in three issues, with the portraits of John F. Kennedy, King Hussein II, and his son, Crown Prince Hassan.

Gibraltar, a British Crown colony, situated on a rocky headland on the southern coast of Spain, overlooking the Gibraltar Straits connecting the Atlantic Ocean and the Mediterranean Sea, issued postage stamps with an unusual shape in 1950. A series of four stamps to commemorate the new constitution depicted the Rock of Gibraltar. The Rock's outline is perforated, and if the other parts of an originally rectangular stamp are separated, the resulting stamp is the shape of the Rock itself.

In addition to their different shapes, stamps also differ in size. The world's smallest stamp was issued in 1856 by Mecklenburg-Schwerin. It is a minute 10 mm by 10 mm. The territory of Bolivar in present-day Columbia issued another tiny stamp in 1863, which measured 10 $\times$ 13 mm.

Above, clockwise from left to right: **Examples of postage-due stamps — Romania, Israel, Austrian Military Post, Great Britain, Brazil, Haiti and Madagascar.**

A postage-due stamp on Czechoslovak mail which was not franked. As the sender did not put a ten-*heller* stamp on this postcard, the recipient had to pay double postage of 20 *hellers.*

Examples of overprinted stamps (*from left to right*): the protectorate Böhmen und Mähren (from Nazi occupation of Czechoslovakia); Germany (Belgian Military Post in the Rhineland); Czechoslovakia (a conversion of a definitive stamp into a postage-due stamp, including a change of nominal value); Austria (a change of nominal value); Ghana (Proclamation of Independence); the German Reich (a conversion of a definitive stamp into an official stamp).

Larger stamps, however, are much more common, especially in France and the former Soviet Union. The largest-ever stamps are the United States newspaper stamps, which were issued in 1865 and measure 52 × 95 mm.

Postage stamps with an unusual 'overprint' with perforation, or perfins. The internationally used term 'perfin' comes from the English '*perf*orated *in*itials'. Perforated postage stamps first appeared in the 1870s. With the approval of postal authorities, companies and firms with large amounts of mail began to use these stamps to prevent the theft and misuse by staff. The perforation takes, for example, the form of one or more letters; numbers or symbols. Stamp collectors considered stamps with perfins as valueless and for a long period disposed of them. At present, however, stamps with perfins are considered to be interesting philatelic material. In addition to the stamps with 'private' perfins of individual companies and firms, there are also stamps with official, postal perfins. The official perforation has a similar function to that of an overprint. It usually changes the postal purpose of these stamps. For example, the Bavarian official stamps for state railways issued between 1912 and 1915 were made from the definitive stamps punched with a perfin in the shape of the letter 'E'.

Stamp-Printing Materials

The first postage stamps that were not printed on stamp paper were Latvian stamps issued between 1918 and 1920. Due to shortage of stamp paper, the stamps were printed on the back of military maps left in Latvia by the German army, and on the back of incomplete sheets of five- and ten-*rouble* banknote paper.

After the Second World War, some countries used metal foils to print stamps. These were either foils with a paper backing, metalized paper, or foils without a paper backing. As foil is very flexible and able to preserve any shape, postage stamps are usually produced by relief printing; the resulting stamps look rather like coins.

Aluminium foil was first used for stamp printing in 1955 in Hungary, commemorating both the 20th anniversary of the Hungarian aluminium industry, and the World Congress on Non-Ferrous Metals.

Gold foil was first used for stamp printing by the kingdom of Tonga, which produced a series of circular stamps commemorating the first Polynesian gold coinage issue. The Republic of Gabon issued similar stamps in honour of Albert Schweitzer, the famous German missionary doctor. A number of overseas countries, especially the French colonies, have issued stamps on gold or silver foil.

Finally, the small Himalayan kingdom of Bhutan issued a series of postage stamps on steel foil

Examples of
pre-cancels: Canada,
US, France, Belgium.

Examples of various
stamp shapes:
Gibraltar,
Czechoslovakia,
Belgium
(a telegraph stamp),
Iraq.

to mark the achievements of her steel industry.

Postage stamps can also be printed on silk. One example is a block issued to commemorate the 400th anniversary of the Polish postal services. The kingdom of Bhutan issued a miniature sheet and a series of stamps on silk; and the post office of Grenada, a small island country in the Lesser Antilles, commemorated Jennifer Hosten, Miss World 1970–1971, by issuing a miniature sheet on silk.

The real reason, however, for issuing stamps on foil or silk is, in fact, the desire to promote interest among stamp collectors. Such stamps are geared towards the philatelic market rather than for routine use in postal operations, where postage stamps printed on special stamp paper are the norm.

Interesting and Unusual Stamps

Collectors' interest in stamps, together with the desire of some postal administrations to increase stamp sales and state revenue, can lead to the issuing of unusual stamps.

The postage stamps of Sierra Leone, a former British colony in Africa, are a typical example. The stamps come in various shapes, resembling a pear, an eagle, a heart, an anvil, and a map of Africa.

In addition to printing postage stamps on steel foil and silk, the Bhutan post office issued other postal curiosa for collectors. It has issued stamps on solid plastic; stamps shaped like miniature

Examples of stamps from
Sierra Leone.

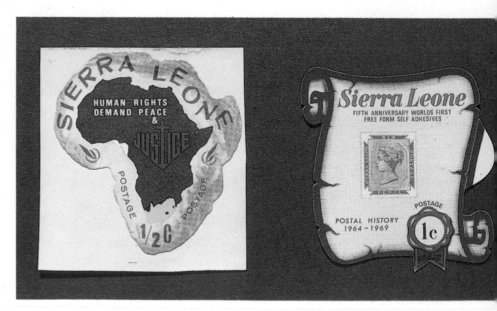

The Sunday stamps issued by the Belgian Post Office between 1893 and 1914. The accompanying coupon bore an inscription in French and Flemish 'No Sunday Delivery'.
The sender indicated if he wished to have the mail delivered on Sunday by tearing off or crossing out the coupon.

records, stereoscopic stamps with three-dimensional views of butterflies, fish, or roses; and scented stamps with various kinds of roses impregnated with rose-water essence. The postal function of these stamps, in these cases, is, however, questionable.

It is little wonder that some of these curious postal stamps are described in the world's stamp catalogues as mint stamps only; the value of used stamps is not given because of the lack of any real information, as it is very difficult indeed to prove the actual use of the stamps in the postal system.

5 Rarities and Single Specimens

In terms of collecting, a 'rarity' is an uncommon object, and as such becomes a collectors' item; a 'single specimen' is a rarity known to exist only singly. While rarities and single specimens are out of the reach of most collectors, collectors nevertheless often wish to see them with their own eyes, just to admire them for a moment. With regret but a certain satisfaction, the collectors happily return to their own collections, and to what they consider their own 'rarities and single specimens'.

Famous Mauritian Issues

Mauritius is an island to the east of Madagascar in the Indian Ocean. Sir William Maynard Gomm had been governor for five years when the first Mauritian postage stamps — the Mauritian Red and Blue — appeared in the year 1847.

Gomm was an experienced army officer, who soon realized how inefficient the island's transport and postal systems were. He was probably familiar with the reformed English postal system, which had adopted adhesive postage stamps as a form of pre-payment for the delivery of letters. Towards the end of 1846, Gomm issued a directive that set postal rates — 1 $^1/_2$ d. for local delivery; 2d. for $^1/_2$-ounce letters delivered throughout the island — and various other rates for overseas post. Gomm decided not to wait for postage stamps to be sent from England, but ordered their printing on the island, even though he did not have experienced engravers and printers, and instead had to use the services of a local clockmaker and jeweller, who was probably chosen because he owned a printing press on which he used to produce visiting cards.

As documented in the British Museum records, Mr Barnard drew the designs of the first two Mauritian stamps and then engraved them on to one copper plate for a fee of £10. He was paid another ten shillings to print 500 copies each of the Mauritius red POST OFFICE and the Mauritius Blue POST OFFICE.

There is a famous story of how the 'printing error' (a postal paper that resulted from a mistake made prior to its printing, but which was nevertheless distributed), Mauritius POST OFFICE, came into existence. It is said that Barnard engraved the head of the Queen first, then the upper inscription POSTAGE, followed by the bottom inscription ONE PENNY or TWO PENNY, respectively, and the inscription MAURITIUS on the right.

As he could not remember the agreed inscription for the left-hand side, he went to see the local postmaster. Before reaching his office, Barnard noticed the sign POST OFFICE, which struck him as quite appropriate for the left-hand side of the stamp, so he returned without consulting the postmaster as intended. He then engraved the left-hand side of the stamps with the inscription POST OFFICE.

While printing the stamps, Barnard began to have doubts about the inscription POST OFFICE, so he again went to consult the postmaster. It is not known what the postmaster's reply was, but tradition has it that Lady Gomm persuaded her husband the governor to give Barnard his word that the whole issue, regardless of the erroneous inscription, would be accepted by the authorities, and paid for!

It is said that Lady Gomm intervened because she wished to use the new stamps on the invitations to her fancy-dress ball, marking the 5th anniversary of her husband's appointment as governor of Mauritius. Barnard finished printing the stamps, and the first Mauritian stamps went on sale on 20 or 21 September 1847. Not surprisingly, Lady

Famous Mauritian issues: the Mauritius Red and Blue on a letter.

About one-quarter of all Mauritian issues are to be found in museums and in the British Royal Stamp Collection. When they are exhibited at big international or world stamp exhibitions, they are greatly admired by philatelists and non-philatelists alike.

The Single Stamp

The 1856 one-cent British Guiana (today Guiana) Red is one of the rarest stamps, and the only one known to exist. It is a black impression on red paper, cancelled with a double circular DEMERARA postmark. Although badly damaged, this stamp is recognized as unique, and the world's most valuable stamp. Because all four corners have been cut off, the resulting shape is octagonal. Some experts consider it to be a 'printing error'. Other experts even doubt its authenticity as such, and do not rule out the possibility that the right-sided inscription FOUR CENTS was changed to the inscription ONE CENT.

Gomm purchased most of the newly issued stamps for her fancy-dress ball invitations. Lady Gomm received her stamps on time, and Governor Gomm received confirmation that his order had been carried out. Barnard received his financial reward, and philatelists were bequeathed two of the world's philatelic rarities.

The present-day owners of these Mauritian issues are with few exceptions well known, regardless of where they live. The discovery of any further specimens would cause great interest not only in philatelic circles, but among the wider public as well. The Mauritius Red has been preserved in two mint and fifteen used specimens, while the Mauritius Blue is known to exist in five mint and nine used specimens. Both stamps, the Mauritius Red and the Mauritius Blue, used on one envelope represent the best-known and most expensive entire. An entire is a letter, an envelope, or a postcard documenting postal services.

The island of Mauritius is part of the Mascarene Islands. It was a British colony from 1810 to 1968 when it gained its independence. Madagascar has been a full-time member of the UPU since 1969.

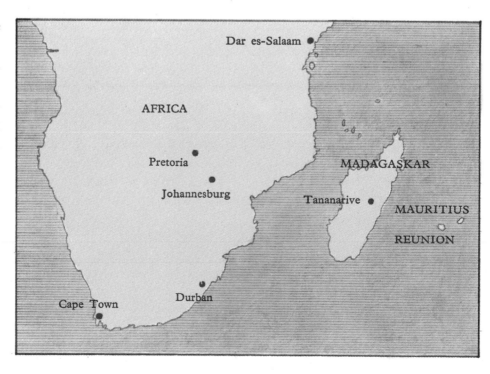

Philippe La Renotière de Ferrari, the legendary 'Postage Stamp King'.

Lucien Vernon Vaughan of Demerara (present-day Georgetown) in British Guiana discovered the 1856 one-cent BG Red in family correspondence around 1873. He wrote about his discovery in an article for the *London Daily Mail* in 1934, describing how strange it felt to know that in his childhood he had once owned this priceless stamp. He had sold it for 6/- (six shillings) sixty-one years previously, and now it was being exhibited at world stamp exhibitions, protected round the clock by security men.

As a small boy Vaughan had been very keen on stamps. He was delighted when once he discovered a pile of family correspondence franked chiefly with British Guianese stamps. The famous one-cent BG Red originally was affixed to an envelope; Vaughan removed it and put it in his album.

The stamp did not stay there for long, however. One day when visiting a stamp dealer in Bath he saw several series of foreign mint stamps that were from countries which he had never heard of before. They were so attractive that Vaughan decided to sell some of his British Guianese stamps and buy the foreign series.

Because he did not consider it to be a good specimen, he checked through his album and took out the one-cent BG Red. Vaughan also believed he could replace it easily with a better specimen. He offered the stamp to Mr N. R. McKinnon, who was known to be an experienced stamp collector. McKinnon did not want the stamp because it was damaged, however he took pity on young Vaughan, who seemed so keen to sell it to him, and gave him 6/- (six shillings), adding that he was taking a huge risk in buying a damaged octagonal stamp.

Several years later Mr McKinnon sold his entire collection, including the one-cent BG Red for £120. Philippe La Renotière de Ferrari, who owned the largest stamp collection in the world at that time, bought the British Guiana. For forty-four years the stamp remained in his collection, which was sold in Paris between 1921 and 1922; Arthur Hind, the American millionaire, bought the British Guiana for $ 32,900.

After Hind's death, his stamp collection was dispersed. The famous stamp was sold to a New York owner in 1940. At present it is valued at several hundred thousand dollars.

As there are rumours about all famous stamps, there are some rumours and stories about this British Guiana. One story is based on an anonymous letter received in 1938 by the American magazine *Stamp and Collectors' Review*, which claimed there was another British Guiana Red in existence.

This story is linked to another about a poor boy who enlisted in the crew of an old passenger steamer. In his home port he had a boyhood friend whom he met occasionally, and who once gave him a pile of old letters, and an envelope filled with stamps that used to belong to his father. His father had intended to become a stamp collector one day, but died before doing anything about his stamps. It is not known what the young sailor felt about his friend's gift as he did not know anything about stamps; he did not get any letters, and he had hardly any money to buy stamps.

It was only years later, when he read newspaper articles about famous stamp collectors such as Ferrari, and Hind and his priceless BG Red, that the sailor realized that one of his stamps looked exactly like it. But when he thought more about the stamp and how lucky he was, he saw that the stamp could land him in trouble: he could not prove how he had acquired the stamp because his boyhood friend was now dead. He did not want to provoke suspicion, or the unwelcome attention of the tax authorities, much less unscrupulous people who might want to share his fortune. And yet he knew it was nearly impossible for him to sell the stamp without immediately attracting the attention of the entire world.

After a time, the sailor found a solution. One day Arthur Hind received a letter telling him that his famous stamp was not the only specimen in existence. The letter hinted that one of the specimens might even have to be destroyed. Mr Hind was offered the choice: to sell his British Guiana or to buy the second specimen. The writer suggested a meeting at which the matter could be discussed discreetly; he also promised to bring his stamp for Mr Hind's inspection.

Mr Hind had no idea of the identity of the second stamp owner, nor how wealthy he might be. As he did not intend to sell his own stamp, he knew that the second British Guiana would have to be destroyed.

When the two stamp owners met in Hind's study, Hind was thrilled when his guest took a small diary out of his pocket and laid it open on the table. Indeed, Hind saw a second 1856 British Guiana Red in front of him. He took a magnifying glass and carefully examined the stamp; it had a fold on the right-hand side, but this was not significant in such a rarity. Hind opened the vault in a corner of his study and took out his own precious stamp.

The two stamp owners spent a long time examining and comparing the two specimens. Neither of them was sure what to do next. Finally, Hind asked the simple question, 'How much?' His guest mentioned a sum, both men shook hands, and the deal was done. Hind promised to have the cash ready the following day.

When the two men met again, the guest put his British Guiana stamp down next to the prepared cash. Hind once again carefully inspected the other stamp, and then put his magnifying glass down with relief: the matter was concluded successfully. Hind is said to have offered a cigar to his guest, and then to have taken one himself. He lit the cigars, picked up his newly acquired stamp, and burned it in the flame of his match. This story only was revealed to the public long after Hind's death.

Present-Day Rarities and Unique Specimens

In addition to the classic rarities and unique specimens, of which the two most famous — the Mauritius Red and Blue and the 1856 one-cent British Guiana Red — are mentioned above, there are other stamps that have been issued since the 1870s. Due to various overprints, the range of these stamps is quite extensive. Collectors are often not so keen on these issues because it is difficult to prove any objective reason for their production, that is, the stamps were issued officially to respond to a real postal need, without the intention of creating a philatelic rarity. This fact, however, does not in any way affect the decision to include most of these overprint issues in stamp catalogues.

A complete survey of postal rarities and single specimens would be rather lengthy because stamps have been issued for over 150 years. The earliest rarities and single specimens are known to exist from the first years of stamp issuing. Some occurred during printing, such as double prints; printing on the face and reverse of the stamps; an error in the inscription or overprint; or the use of a wrong dye or wrong stamp paper.

Other examples are classic stamps in blocks of four, large blocks, such as a unique thirty-eight block of New South Wales 3*d.* of 1852, or even whole sheets

Above: **Valuable Czechoslovak rarities — the overprint** Pošta československá **on the Austrian definite stamps from 1916—1918: a four-crown Czechoslovak stamp, light-green, granite paper, broad format, type I; a four-crown Czechoslovak stamp, light-green, granite paper, borad format, type II, inverted overprint; a ten-crown Czechoslovak stamp, violet, granite paper, broad format, type II.**

Left: **A unique stamp — the one-cent British Guiana Red.**

in which stamps were distributed to post offices.

One of the most popular rarities is due to a printing error: the 1918 United States twenty-four cent airmail stamp in blue and red with its centre inverted. As there are about eighty specimens in existence, this stamp should not really be considered a world rarity, but it is, because of its special popularity among collectors. It was issued on 13 May 1918 to commemorate the first scheduled flight between Washington D. C. and New York via Philadelphia, on 15 May 1918.

A Washington D. C. bank clerk and a keen philatelist bought an entire sheet of this stamp at its nominal value. When he spotted the printing error, he sold the sheet for $15,000. Soon after the sheet was sold for $20,000 to another New York collector. Some time later this collector divided the sheet into a block of eight and three blocks of four, and sold the rest as single stamps, initially at a price of $250 and later rising to $500 or more. It is believed that about twenty specimens were destroyed. Present-day American catalogues value a single specimen of this stamp at a price of $12,000.

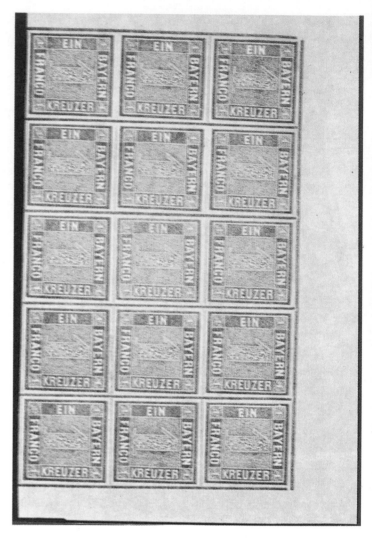

Bavarian 'No. 1', a block of fifteen — the first German postage stamp.

6 *The Post Office Today*

Modern Postage Stamp Designs

From the very first issue of British stamps, for nearly half a century postage stamps had a single function, namely a postal function. Consequently, stamp designs during that period were not particularly original, primarily promoting national sovereignty, whether of an independent country or a colony, and showing the definite value of the stamp. The portrait of a current sovereign, the national coat-of-arms, an al-legorical design, a postal symbol, or a simple numeral giving the value were the most common stamp designs.

The first attempts to be more creative appeared soon afterwards in other countries, but mainly in the United States. In 1869 that country issued postage stamps incorporating in their designs a locomotive, a postal steamer, and a galloping pony. A Guatemalan stamp from the same period bears the picture of a parrot. But these designs were rather exceptional; the graphic design of stamps was subject to their postal function. In common with banknotes, the fine quality of stamp-engraving served primarily to prevent forgery, while at the same time creating an aesthetic impression. Many more primitively engraved stamps were issued at this time as well.

Postal administrations gradually realized that stamps could be used for non-postal purposes too, in particular for propaganda and publicity reasons. This led to the issuing of commemorative stamps, the first one being issued

Examples of modern postage stamp designs.

The Columbus Day series issued by the US Post Office in 1893 to commemorate the discovery of America.

in Peru in 1871, to mark the opening of the Chorillos-Lima-Callao railway line. In addition to its definitive value (five *centavos*) and the place names, the stamp also incorporates a locomotive and the Peruvian coat-of-arms in its design. Additional information, such as the date of the railway line opening, is not given, a shortcoming that was later corrected when other countries began to issue their own commemorative stamps. One important date marked by commemorative stamps was the 400th anniversary of Christopher Columbus's landing in America. Nicaragua and Honduras each issued a series of stamps in 1892. A year later, the United States and Salvador followed their example. The Dominican Republic commemorated Christopher Columbus Day several years later.

The large, sixteen-stamp Co-lumbus Day series issued by the United States post office astounded stamp collectors. Most countries were rather conservative in their stamp issues, and often would not alter their stamp designs for years. When collectors began to scrutinize the Columbus series, however, they were disappointed. Each stamp depicts Columbus differently: the stamp showing him as the expedition's leader depicts him as a young, beardless man at the prow of his ship surrounded by his crew, observing the long-awaited landfall; but the stamp depicting his first steps on the North American continent shows him with a beard. Indeed, the time that elapsed between these two events cannot have been long enough for Columbus to grow a beard! Similar discrepancies can be observed on the other stamps. (By way of excusing the

United States post office, it is important to add that the stamps were reproduced from paintings that had become famous long before someone came up with the idea of depicting the events on postage stamps.)

At the beginning of the 20th century, some European postal administrations issued fascinating commemorative stamps which successfully merged the propaganda function of a stamp with sophisticated design. The earliest charity stamps also date from this period, while the first airmail stamps appeared towards the end of the First World War.

The end of the War was responsible for profound changes in the world. New stamp-issuing countries came into existence, and the structure of colonial powers changed. These changes are reflected in various philatelists' albums.

The period between the First and Second World Wars was characterized by a sharp increase in the numbers of commemorative and airmail issues appearing for propaganda purposes, and even for the philatelists themselves. Stamps with tablets (printed or blank sheets of paper attached to stamps) appeared at this time, and a new type of printing arrangement — the so-called miniature sheet — was introduced. A miniature sheet is a commemorative issue consisting of several stamps, although a single-stamp miniature sheet is also issued, with a commemorative inscription or design.

Stamps incorporating new topics were issued which did not go unnoticed. It could be said that the origins of thematic philately date from this inter-war period.

Postage stamps with tablets.

tion REICHSPOST ('Imperial Post'), and later with DEUTSCHES REICH ('German Empire'). This was re-issued several times, and with an additional overprint these stamps were valid throughout German-occupied Poland, Belgium, Latvia, Lithuania, Estonia, Rumania, Holstein, and the French Saarland. The German postal authorities in China, Morocco, and Turkey also used overprinted Germania issues. The fi-

Examples of commemorative sheets issued by the former Soviet Union (*above*) and Switzerland (*below*).

'Permanent' Stamp Designs

While postal administrations endeavour to issue stamps with wide-ranging designs, many issues still preserve traditional designs for many years.

In Imperial Germany at the turn of the century, festivals and pageants were popular that centred on Germania, a personification of the country. Anna Führing, a publican's daughter and actress, became famous when she acted in the role of Germania during the centenary celebrations in honour of the first modern German Emperor and Prussian king, Wilhelm I (1797–1888).

It is a little wonder that Paul Waldraff, a painter and graphic designer, asked her to become his model for a postage stamp depicting the allegorical Germania.

The Germania issue first appeared in 1900 with the inscrip-

nal Germania reissue was produced in 1922.

Another good example of a permanent stamp motif is the 'Semeuse' ('The Sower') on a popular French stamp. The French post office issued it for the first time in 1903, and the final issue appeared in 1938. Some stamps remained, which were overprinted three years later with the 1941 value. This stamp was designed by N. Roty, a Parisian sculptor, and engraved by E. Mouchon.

N. Roty spotted the model for the 'Semeuse' selling vegetables at an Auvergne village market. He liked her face so much that he made a pencil sketch of it. Soon afterwards, when working on a medal for a major agricultural exhibition, Roty used the portrait of this pretty market-trader on one of the sides.

In 1897 the French Ministry of Finance held a competition to design a fifty *centimes* coin. Roty took part, and his design — which was in fact the slightly altered agricultural medal — won first prize. The new coins with the market girl's portrait were distributed throughout France. The pretty girl herself unknowingly handled the fifty *centimes* coins bearing her own portrait.

When the French post office

A book of stamps with the *Semeuse* ('The Sower') issued by the French Post Office

decided to issue new postage stamps it held a competition, and Roty was once again successful. In 1903 the first five definitive stamps with the 'Semeuse' were issued. Some critics argued that the new stamps were illogical as the woman's fluttering hair and dress seemed to indicate she was sowing against the wind. However, thousands of French citizens saw in her the symbol of 'La Belle France', declaring it was indeed the Sower's historical mission to go against the wind, since she was, after all, disseminating noble ideas.

Another example of a permanent motif is the Portuguese definitive stamp of a woman holding a sickle; in stamp catalogues the woman is referred to as the goddess Ceres. Her picture can be found on 157 Portuguese definitive stamps, and also on the Portuguese colonial stamps of the period. Thus, the complete collection consists of nearly 750 stamps, all bearing precisely the same principal motif.

The Finnish heraldic lion is also an example of a permanent motif. It appeared on the first Finnish stamp in 1856 when Finland was an autonomous part of tsarist Russia; it can still be seen today, 131 years later, on the 1987 Finnish stamp.

Postage stamps with 'permanent' motifs.

Printing Errors

A mistake or fault that occurs during printing results in what is known as a 'printing error'. Philatelists distinguish between a printing error caused by a variation in colour, an incorrect overprint of a colour or its use on the wrong stamp or an inappropriate stamp paper used with a wrong watermark.

More interesting printing errors might occur when stamps are printed in two stages, that is, when the frame and the centre of the stamp are printed separately. In such cases the centre might be inverted in relation to the frame, or different denominations might be included in the frame and in the centre. However, these print-ing errors are rare because they are usually detected at the inspection stage and are not distributed, which is why such errors are considered collectors' items.

Aware of the serious nature of their stamp issuing, postal administrations may take steps to prevent a printing error from becoming a valuable rarity. The United States post office once issued a stamp with the portrait of Dag Hammarskjöld, the UN Secretary-General who had been tragically killed in an air crash. During printing, a mistake was made that aroused a great deal of interest among the public. A certain Mr Leonard Shermann discovered a printing error in a small section of the issue: the yellow network had been repro-duced upside down. The Press began to write about the printing error, referring to the stamp as a world rarity. Mr Shermann himself received tempting offers asking him to sell his stamps singly or by the sheet. However, his dreams about getting rich quick were shattered by an unexpected decision by the United States postmaster general, who ordered a reprint of the imperfect stamp. In a few days the public were able to buy these imperfect stamps in any quantity they wished at their definitive value at post office counters. More than forty million of this 'rarity' had been issued, and was sold out quickly to bargain hunters.

Printing errors have to be considered as a separate category from those stamps that have been badly engraved, or entire issues that have been printed with a mistake due to the designer's ineptitude, inattention, or ignorance.

Although the design of each stamp is checked by a number of people, mistakes do occur. For instance, in 1903 the St Kitts-Nevis Islands in the Lesser Antilles belatedly issued a stamp commemorating the 400th anniversary of Columbus Day, with Christopher Columbus holding a pair of binoculars. The stamp's designer cannot have realized that binoculars were discovered only much later after Christopher Columbus' time.

The Polish post office issued a series of stamps to commemorate the 15th anniversary of the United Nations Children's Fund, UNICEF. One stamp depicts a woman with a child holding a milk bottle; the bottle leans to one side, but its contents appear to defy the laws of physics.

A First Day Cover with a block of four US stamps issued in 1961 to mark the death of Dag Hammarskjöld, the UN Secretary-General, plus a printing error of the same stamp (yellow missing around the UN headquarters).

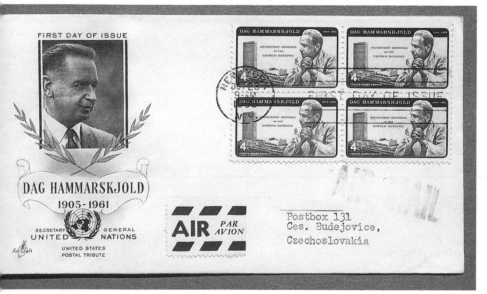

Above, from left to right: Printing errors: the then East German stamp issued to mark the centenary of the death of Robert Schumann (1810—1856) with musical notation: a) incorrect, b) correct; the 1956 Italian stamp commemorating the 50th anniversary of the Simplon rail tunnel.

The then East German post office issued two stamps to mark the centenary of Robert Schumann's death. In addition to the composer's portrait, the stamps were to have included an example of his work in the form of musical notes. Instead, samples of Franz Schubert's work were given. Some time later the stamps were reissued with the correct musical notation.

The post office of the Republic of Mali cannot have been pleased when their 'Chess Championship' stamp series wrongly depicted a crossword puzzle in place of a chessboard.

An interesting and a remarkable story is linked to the Italian stamp issued in the 1950s commemorating the 50th anniversary of the Simplon Rail Tunnel. When the stamp appeared, it caused some amusement and was also highly criticized. Critics pointed to several discrepancies: primarily, the stamp had a picture of a puffing steam locomotive pulling a number of coaches, but the Simplon Rail Tunnel had, in fact, been electrified since its inception. As well, the tunnel traffic runs on the left-hand side track, whereas on the stamp the train leaving the tunnel uses the right-hand track.

The Italian post office ordered an investigation, and the conclusions were surprising. Evidently, the ceremonial opening of the Simplon Rail Tunnel and then the inaugural train journey did not take place on the same day. The ceremonial opening actually took place on 1 June 1906, and marked the completion of the first of two tunnels. It was only provisional, and before the tunnel itself became fully operational a special commission had to inspect whether it conformed to safety regulations. A steam train was used for this maiden journey so the remaining electrification work would not be interrupted. According to the commission report, the steam train went through the tunnel for the first and last time more than three months after the official opening. The train also used the wrong track, until then unelectrified. This track was in fact electrified and made fully operational only seventeen years later.

This historical inaugural journey was captured in a photograph enclosed with the commission report. The stamp designer used this photograph, thinking that it had recorded the Tunnel's ceremonial opening. The public accepted this, and the stamp remained valid, even though today's reality is, in fact, very different from the picture on the stamp.

7 A Philatelic Collection

Collecting is a matter of individual interest that satisfies the collector. Collecting is mainly a personal matter: one can collect whatever he or she wants, in whatever manner, if it provides satisfaction. This principle particularly applies in philately.

Over more than one hundred years of philatelic history, certain principles of stamp collecting have been adopted. These come from experience that has been acquired by earlier generations of philatelists, and from the study of philatelic material.

Philately is divided into the following categories: traditional philately, thematic philately, philately, postal history, postal stationery, and maximaphily.

Most collectors devote themselves to traditional philately, that is, collecting stamps of indi-

Examples of analogous postcards: Luxembourg — Victor Hugo, the French poet, playwright and novelist (1802—1885); Hungary — the 18th century Kazan icon.

Another example of analogous postcards: the Soviet Union — the *Ochakov* cruiser from 1922.

vidual stamp-issuing countries. The term 'stamp-issuing countries' might not be understood fully by non-philatelists, and even by some philatelists themselves. It is the traditional term designating any country that issues its own postage stamps and participates in the international postal network. It is unimportant whether it is a large or a small country, or a territory that is independent or dependent. In general, it might be said that the inscription on the stamp designates the stamp-issuing country (see Chapter 2, 'The Introduction of Postage Stamps', for exceptions in which the name of the stamp-issuing country is missing). For instance, the United Nations and the Thurn-Taxis postal territory are regarded as stamp-issuing countries.

Thematic philately differs from all the other branches of philately because in addition to applying the philatelic principles, it also requires specialized knowledge of a particular topic.

Aerophilately embraces collections of stamps and postal items relating to airmail post. In recent years, astrophilately has become a branch related to aerophilately that is concerned with collecting and studying postal items that have been conveyed by spacecraft. The entires that were carried experimentally on board the first space rockets will undoubtedly become the 'classics' of this branch of philately. However, astrophilately awaits further developments, which will come with the future advancement of 'space postal services'.

Postal history as a branch of philately includes collections of philatelic material related to philatelic history such as postmarks, and material on special kinds and ways of conveying postal items and messages.

Collections of postal stationery include envelopes, postcards, letter-cards, and postal wrappers, etc., for newspapers and magazines with an impressed postage stamp, although a picture or a design might replace the stamp.

Maximaphily involves collecting postcards depicting the same subjects as the stamps attached to them. These stamps have to be cancelled by the appropriate postmark, usually of a commemorative nature. These postcards are called maximum cards. Maximaphily is a collecting trend that is especially popular in France and the United States.

Collections related to traditional philately, postal history, postal stationery, and aerophilately (including astrophilately), might be general, specialized, or study collections. Thematic collections form an independent category.

A general collection contains all standard stamps, and postal stationery or postmarks in chronological order as they were issued or distributed, without any regard for deviations or peculiarities. The standard of such a collection depends on the condition of the stamps or any postal material, and especially the completeness of all standard issues or postal stationery according to any general stamp catalogue that does not contain reference to printing or usage irregularities.

A specialized collection is based on a detailed elaboration of a general collection, or a detailed study of one of its parts. It usually includes stamps or other philatelic material from one stamp-issuing country, or from only one period of its postal activity. The collector pays attention to any peculiarity that occurs during printing or usage, such as varieties, printing errors,

Examples of stamps with a shifted centre (*above*), and a diagram of how they are created through an error in perforation (*below*).

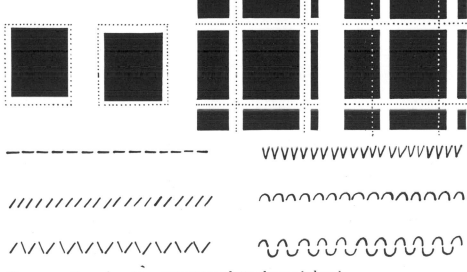

The separation of postage stamps: roulette shapes (*above*).

Types of perforation (*below*): a) Line perforation is the earliest and the simplest method. A perforation machine punches each stamp row separately, both horizontally and vertically. b) Comb perforation. The perforation comb-punches perforations on three sides of each row of stamps, for example the upper side and two lateral sides. The sheet of stamps is then moved one row up and the second strike creates the remaining perforation on the bottom side of the first row of stamps, which is simultaneously the upper side of the second row, and the two lateral sides of the second row. This procedure is repeated until all rows of stamps have been perforated. c) Harrow perforation. This is the most advanced method as the whole sheet of stamps is punched at a single stroke, making the stamp edges regular.

watermarks, methods of separating stamps (cutting, perforation, or other), or stamp-dies. It takes time and a fair degree of experience and patience to compile a specialized collection; indeed, it often becomes a collector's lifelong endeavour.

A thematic collection differs from those mentioned above because the collector chooses to devote him- or herself to a specialized topic by selecting the most relevant philatelic material. On the one hand the material illustrates the topic, for example, by using stamps whose pictures relate to it, on the other hand it also documents the topic by content, place, or date of origin.

Maximaphily collections relate to stamp-issuing countries, and can be specialized, study, or thematic collections.

The collector who decides to show the results of years of collecting at a stamp exhibition first has to prepare a philatelic exhibit. He or she must have a clear idea of what to exhibit. This is stated in the introduction of the exhibit (or in the catalogue), and an appropriate title is given on the front page. As any collection is always more representative than any selected exhibit, it is necessary to choose the most appropriate material.

These remarks apply equally to young philatelists, although the individual requirements are graded according to age.

How to Collect Stamps

There is no type of work that can be done successfully without the necessary tools and equipment. An engineer has certain tools,

Unperforated stamps have to be separated by cutting. The Austrian stamp shown above was first issued perforated, however, the remaining sheets were distributed unperforated because the printers could not meet the demands for stamps at post office counters.

ence. A proper pair of philatelic tweezers has oblong, flattened ends. Surgical or cosmetic tweezers, with either pointed or indented ends, are completely unsuitable and should never be used to handle stamps.

The second basic tool is a magnifying glass. An ordinary magnifying glass with 3× or 4× magnitude is adequate for examining stamps. However, magnifying glasses with 8× or 10× magnitude are more suitable for identifying minute details or studying inscriptions. The so-called lumin-

escent magnifying glasses that are equipped with a small bulb have become popular.

A stock box is used for storing stamps before they are mounted in a proper album. It can also be used to hold surplus stamps or other philatelic items. It contains dark or white sheets with transparent foil strips, under which stamps are inserted.

A stamp album obviously is indispensable. It is possible to buy general albums of individual stamp-issuing countries. The album sheets contain pre-printed

Examples of philatelic material which form part of specialized collections: a) An example of denoting differences in stamps of the same kind and denomination to differentiate their types (type I: 14 pearls in the frame of the stamp's picture; type II: 19 pearls). b) Gutters — empty, or at times printed strips of paper dividing two counter sheets, appear if large sheets come to a postal counter uncut into the so-called 'counter' or 'post office' sheets (panes). c) Plate marks provide information on the number of printing plates used to print a stamp. d) A coloured testing scale, which is used for automatic checking of intaglio printing plates. e) Specimens of stamps issued in sheets and in stamp rolls for automatic slot machines. f) A stamp issued in roll form, perforated on all four sides but smaller in size than the same stamp issued in sheet form. g) Row control-numbers (an example of a sheet of German stamps from the inflationary period after the First World War). They stated the total nominal value of stamps in either individual rows or columns, and helped to speed up the calculation of postage.

while a writer needs a pen or a typewriter; the philatelist also requires special equipment.

A pair of philatelic tweezers is the most important tool. A stamp should never be touched with bare fingers because this can leave oily or wet marks on mint stamps; stamps can also get dirty or can be damaged easily. Using a pair of tweezers is simple, it merely requires some experi-

b

c

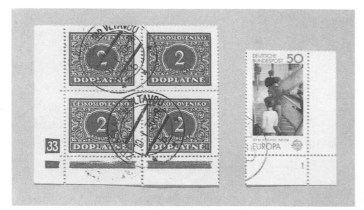

e

a

d

f

g

grids for individual stamps, which are often illustrated or have their catalogue numbers given. These provide guidance on which stamps to collect, and how to arrange them. General albums are supplemented with loose leaves for storing stamps issued in the previous year. Loose album sheets are also provided for collecting mint stamps, which are not mounted permanently on to a sheet, but are inserted under a transparent foil that covers each stamp grid. The collector preparing an exhibit usually uses loose album sheets without any bottom print, that is, without pre-printed stamp grids.

Cancelled stamps are mounted permanently, but differently from mint stamps because they are normally attached to an envelope or a postcard. Small philatelic hinges made of transparent paper with gum on one side are used.

A postage-stamp catalogue is an important and indispensable guide for the less-experienced — as well as the experienced — collector. The catalogue facilitates recognition of the stamp, and provides important and interesting details and includes a list of stamps issued by each individual stamp-issuing country, or stamp-issuing countries in any one continent. Stamps are arranged chronologically, according to their date of issue.

In addition to depicting individual stamps and sometimes their details, the catalogue usually provides further information, such as characteristic features of varieties; details on stamp-dies; the kind and size of perforation; the watermark used; the designer and engraver of a stamp; the date of issue; and the date of val-

idity. The scope of information depends on whether it is a general or a specialized catalogue. Most catalogues also give a brief mention of the stamp design, for example, a landscape, a personality, or a plant.

The catalogue also gives the price of unused stamps in the first column, and used stamps in the second column. Some catalogues provide three or four column evaluations. Here, the first column gives the price of mint,

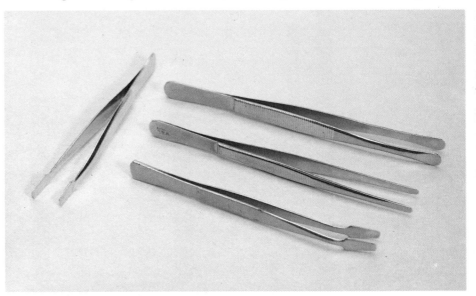

hingeless stamps; the second refers to unused, hinged stamps; the third cancelled stamps; and the fourth column shows the price of stamps affixed to entires.

Once the philatelist becomes more involved in stamp collecting, he or she will start using a stamp catalogue, and sooner or later will come across a stamp whose watermark or perforation will have to be discovered.

As noted earlier, a watermark is a sign such as a drawing or an

Above: **Philatelic tweezers.** *Below:* **Philatelic magnifying glasses.**

Collecting Used and Mint Stamps

A stamp stock-book.

In its earliest stages, the 1860s, philately was concerned only with used stamps. Unused or mint stamps cost money, and therefore only when they had been cancelled by a postmark could they find their way into the collections of the early philatelic pioneers. Collectors were given stamps by friends and acquaintances, and would never contemplate buying mint stamps for their collections.

However, when stamp dealers became established businesses, philatelists suddenly realized how many stamps, and sometimes quite expensive ones, were missing from their collections. They tried to arrange for friends who were abroad to send them stamps, and even became interested in possessing stamps the moment they were issued, including mint stamps. However, the number of used stamps in contemporary collections resulted in a feeling among collectors that only used, cancelled stamps were worth collection.

The popularity of mint stamps increased greatly when dealers started to supply the philatelic market with increased numbers of unused stamps. They also stocked currently issued mint stamps, the collecting of which was simpler and not so time-consuming as collecting used stamps.

A short glance through most catalogues reveals that some stamps, and especially miniature sheets, command the same price whether they are cancelled or not. Indeed, some uncancelled German stamps of the greatly in-

ornament that is included in the stamp paper and is impressed in the paper during the manufacturing process. It becomes visible when held against the light or when placed in a benzene bath. The watermark is used to protect stamps and postal stationery against forgery.

Some catalogues describe watermarks seen from the face (imprinted) stamp side, while other view watermarks from the reverse side. Watermarks can also be positioned differently depending on how the stamp paper was fed into the printing press.

Watermarks can be ascertained professionally using a variety of equipment, some of it rather expensive. The philatelist, however, can use a simple method if the watermark cannot be seen clearly when held against the light or a black background. The stamp is put face-down on a black bakelite or glass tray that contains several drops of clear benzene. The stamp will adhere to the black surface and the wa-

termark will become clearly visible. The stamp will soon dry, without being damaged in any way. A brief immersion in benzene also leaves the gum of mint stamps intact, but some soluble dies could be affected; stamp catalogues generally warn collectors about any potential risks which may be involved.

A perforation gauge is another important tool for the specialized collector. It is used if the stamp issue includes a variety that used a different perforation, making it rare and valuable. In such a case, the perforation is an important differentiating feature.

When looking at the perforation gauge, it becomes clear that the holes made when perforating stamp sheets are of different sizes. The perforation gauge is calibrated to show how many perforation holes are punched over two centimetres. The philatelist can easily establish the gauge if he gradually moves the stamp in relation to this perforating gauge.

flated post-1919 period are of little value, while ordinary cancelled stamps, usually attached to entires, are much more valuable. These should, however, be distinguished from the stamps struck with a cancellation on request of a collector.

Thematic collectors prefer mint stamps because the stamp design can often be obscured by a postmark. Traditional collectors often favour used stamps on entires to have evidence of their postal usage, as well as collecting mint stamps.

The History of the Postmark

Owing to a lack of historical evidence, it is difficult to document precisely why the first postmarks were invented. Envelopes were not widely used in the 17th and 18th centuries. A letter was written on a single sheet of paper, which was then folded over and sealed with wax. The name and address of the recipient was written in the front side. The date, which was often included in the text, makes it possible for us today to ascertain when the letter was posted.

As a rule, the postage due on a letter was decided by its weight and the distance carried. It is likely that the sender was obliged to write down the place from which the letter was dispatched, but as this requirement was quite often not met, the postmasters probably had to enter the name of their post offices in letters. This must have proved time-consuming for the bigger post offices, which resulted in the use of name stamps. These were more convenient and faster to apply than handwriting. French and English name stamps appeared before the end of the 17th century, while in America they appeared in the mid-18th century.

Name-stamps give the place name in a straight line. In France and Austria place names are often preceded by *'de'* or *'von'* ('from') for example *'de* Bayonne', *von* or *v.* /PRAG, which are reminiscent of aristocratic titles (F. R. *de* Chateaubriand, J. W. *von* Goethe). These particular postmarks are also known to collectors as aristocratic postmarks.

The earliest postmarks did not include the date. Because there were increasing complaints concerning postal delays due to postmasters' carelessness, namestamps were soon improved to include the day and month, and later also the year, of posting. A 'date' stamp was also introduced, in response to public criticism of the postal services in Britain in the second half of the

A sheet for a general stamp collection.

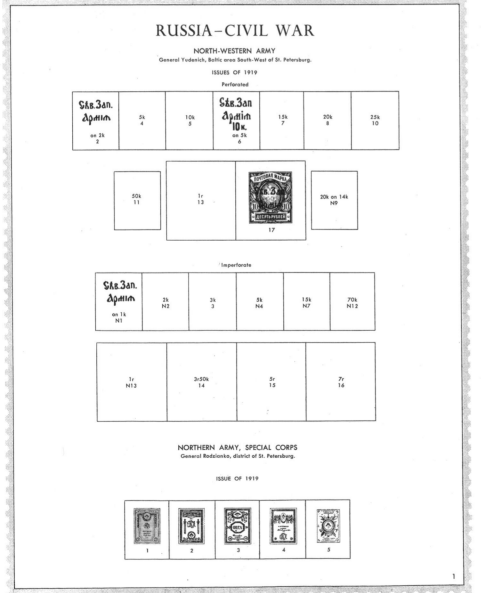

Left: **Affixing stamps on to sheets using hinges.**

Below: **Examples of classical watermarks — Bavaria, Great Britain, Modena, Spain, Argentina.**

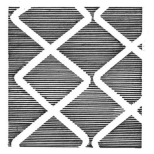

Above: **Examples of watermarks of the 1980s — West Germany, East Germany, Nigeria, Soviet Union, Uruguay.**

Above: Ascertaining a watermark by using benzene.

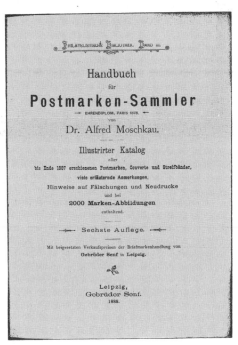

The title page of *A Stamp Collector's Handbook* by the German philatelist Dr Alfred Moschkau (1848—1912).

17th century, by the postmaster general Henry Bishop.

These postmarks are known as pre-stamp postmarks, which are struck on pre-stamp letters. In some countries these postmarks and letters are called, less precisely, 'pre-philatelic'.

The terms 'pre-stamp' postmarks and 'pre-stamp' letters do not refer to the same chronological period for all countries, but depend on when the first postage stamps were issued in each country. For instance, Austrian postmarks were pre-philatelic until 1850, while British postmarks can be considered pre-philatelic only until 1840, as the first British stamps appeared ten years before the first Austrian stamps were issued.

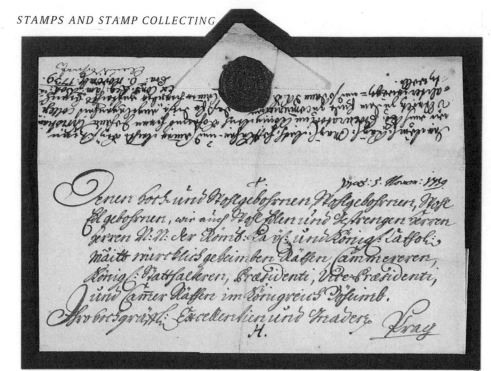

Postmarks provided evidence of official handling by the post office, which undertook the responsibility for delivering letters to respective addresses. They also recorded that the mail was conveyed by the general post and not by a private carrier, which was often the case (individual countries tried to eliminate private carriers through adopting various measures).

Some of the countries that began to issue stamps in the mid-19th century introduced special cancelling or obliterating stamps in addition to the existing name stamps. In the beginning, these cancelling stamps did not bear inscriptions or information; they consisted only of distinctive circles, dots, or diagrams arranged to form various geometric patterns. They are known to philatelists as 'mute cancellations'. They were struck directly on to postage stamps, while the date

Top: A pre-stamp era letter sent to Prague on 6 November 1739.

Above: A pre-stamp era letter sent from Cardenas to Matanzas on 24 March 1848.

Right: Examples of mute cancellations.

Examples of numeral obliterations.

128
LUBECK
B.DE L'ELBE

PRAG

Prag
27. FEB.

Examples of linear cancellations: France (of occupation) and Austria.

stamp — showing the time and place of posting — was situated next to the stamp or on the back of the envelope.

The postmark used to obliterate the first British stamps is a mute cancellation, mistakenly known as the 'Maltese Cross'. In fact, it was originally derived from a four-petalled Tudor rose, and is only vaguely reminiscent of a Maltese Cross.

The most interesting obliterator was introduced in Sicily when stamps with the portrait of King Ferdinand II (1810–1859) were issued. The King, who could not bear the idea that his portrait would be 'defaced' or 'dishonoured' by a cancelling postmark, ordered the use of a special obliterator that framed his stamp portrait rather than obliterating his features.

Some countries used mute cancellations that had a pattern with numbers in the centre. Each post office was allotted a number, according to which the place where the stamp was cancelled could be established, even on loose stamps which had been removed from envelopes. Numeral obliterators were used by postal administrations in Great Britain, the Netherlands, France, Russia, Denmark, and Bavaria.

Lots of the earliest pre-philatelic name stamps were used at many post offices, even after the introduction of postage stamps. They were usually struck as ancillary postmarks, for example, to cancel postal forms. These circular name-postmarks, which were common on some British and French pre-stamp letters, were gradually introduced to other countries.

When Britain introduced postage stamps, initially postmasters were ordered to cancel them in

Stamps for daily cancellations (*above*), and roller cancellers to mark bulky mail or uneven-surfaced mail (*below*).

red ink. As it was possible to wash off this colour quite easily and re-use the stamp, one year later a deep black colour was substituted for the red.

It is likely that initially the colour of the postmark was not considered important by postmasters. Letters from the second half of the 18th century have postmarks in black, red, and brown, with blue being the exception. Later, even green postmarks appeared.

At present, black is the usual colour, although other colours might be used with special cancellations, machine cancels, and explanatory and charge stamps, which are usually made of rubber. Explanatory and charge stamps are used for specific and informative purposes. In contrast to standard stamps, they are used on postal items when required. Some of these explanatory postmarks already appear on pre-stamp envelopes. For example, the postmarks FRANCO or P.P. ('Port Payé') meant that postage was pre-paid by the sender. This was a very important piece of information, because as a rule postage was paid by the recipient. In England the postmark TOO LATE was struck on letters that had to be retained at the post office until the following day.

A French cancel 'Daguin' of 1884.

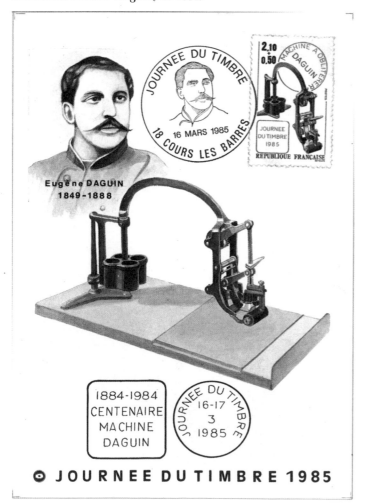

Examples of commemorative post-marks: *opposite page, from top to bottom* — Czechoslovakia, Great Britain, China, Cuba, Germany; *this page, from left to right and to bottom* — Norway, Canada, Austria, Hong Kong, San Marino.

The introduction of postage stamps, which replaced the former cumbersome system of collecting postage, resulted in the universal development of postal systems, including new services and transport methods. These led to the appearance of special postmarks, such as maritime, railway, pneumatic post, and airmail, to record that mail was transported by these carriers.

Important national and public anniversaries, as well as cultural, economic, and sporting events were marked by commemorative postmarks. The first commemorative postmarks appeared in the second half of the 19th century, and became widespread after the Second World War.

Slogan postmarks, which with pictures or inscriptions promote and advertise landmarks and scenery, exhibitions, and various products, are also quite common. These cancellations have been in use for many years in Switzerland, Great Britain, France, and the United States.

In conclusion, meter-marks should be mentioned. Here the meter-mark of an automatic machine replaces the adhesive stamp altogether by printing that postage had been paid. It is usually struck in red, although other colours may be used. The meter-mark incorporates the definitive value, the date, and the user's designation. Sometimes it bears an advertisement, a picture, or some other information. Metered mail machines were first used in Norway, then in New Zealand, and then in the United States at the turn of this century. Since the 1924 Stockholm Postal Union Congress authorized their international use, they have spread to other countries.

Postal Stationery

The term 'postal stationery' refers to any postal paper (a generic term for postage stamps and

A Czechoslovak publicity postmark to commemorate the 1935 Central European Cup Final AC Sparta v. Ferencvaros.

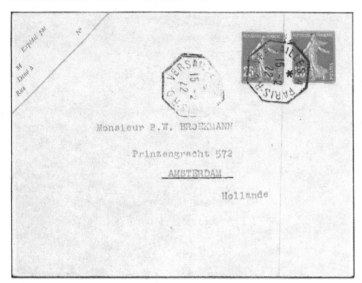

An 1869 Austrian postcard — the world's first postcard (*above*).

An 1897 commemorative Swedish postcard (*above*) issued on the 25th anniversary of King Oscar the Second's accession to the throne (1872—1907).

Postal stationery usually bears impressed definitive stamps. This is illustrated by an envelope (*top left*) issued by the French Post Office and a definitive stamp with the identical illustration from the impressed stamp. However, postal stationery with impressed original stamps is also issued, as illustrated by two envelopes (*centre and bottom left*). One of them commemorates George Washington, the first American president. The second envelope was issued to mark the 40th Anniversary of the French Squadron Normandie-Niemen, established in the Soviet Union during the Second World War.

postal stationery) with an impressed stamp which might be replaced by an illustration or inscription. Postal stationery includes such items as envelopes, letter sheets, letter cards, aerogrammes, and wrappers for newspapers and other periodicals.

The world's first postal stationery was issued in Great Britain in 1840, simultaneously with the first postage stamps. These were the 'Mulready' envelopes and letter sheets, which had to be withdrawn from distribution several months later because they were disliked and laughed at by the public. The failure of the 'Mulready' envelopes did not, however, discourage subsequent designers of postal stationery. In 1841 two more envelopes with the embossed portrait of Queen Victoria were issued. They were received favourably, and set the fashion for many other countries, which issued embossed similar postal stationery.

Another type of postal stationery is the stamped postcard, which appeared in Austria upon the recommendation of Dr Emanuel Herrmann, a professor of economics. In January 1869 Herrmann printed his proposal in the Viennese *Neue Freie Presse*. This was adopted with minor changes, and on 1st October of that year, Austrian and Hungarian post offices began to sell the stamped postcard.

The reverse side of the postcard was used for a short message, whose content could be reproduced or publicized without compromising postal privacy. For example, these messages would state the date of visitors' arrival, requests to forward lost property, business circulars and orders, and so on. The reverse side also bore the disclaimer: 'The Post Office does not accept any responsibility in relation to the content of a message.'

A commemorative postcard issued by San Marino to mark the 1983 Conference of Railwaymen-Philatelists [*top*]. A 1987 commemorative Czechoslovak postcard marking the 100th anniversary of the Czech Philatelic Club in Prague [*above*].

Right: An 1893 commemorative French postcard issued to mark the Russian navy's visit to Toulon.

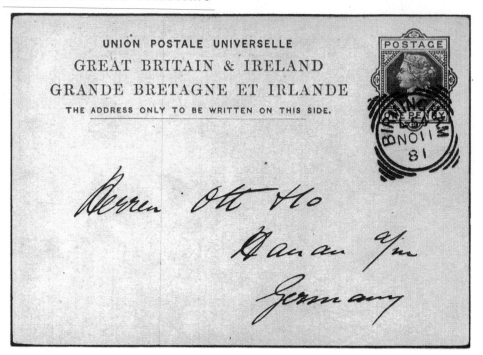

A postcard from Great Britain and Ireland.

similar proposal by the German postmaster general Heinrich von Stephan to issue 'a postal sheet with an embossed definitive stamp' had been refused as an unsuitable type of public communication.

After 1869, stamped postcards were soon introduced to other countries. Initially they were used within the boundaries of one country, but in July 1875 the Universal Postal Union authorized their use internationally. At first, there was no international agreement on the arrangement of the postcard's address side. Later, the Rome Postal Union Con-

The postcard was impressed with a yellow stamp bearing the portrait of the Emperor Franz Joseph I (1830—1916), and had the definitive value of two *kreuzer*. These stamped postcards were popular because they saved on postage and paper, doing away with the need for adhesive stamps; three million were sold in the first three months.

Stamped postcards, together with other types of postal stationery — Austria itself had nearly thirty types — meant a significant simplification of postal operations. Some types of postal stationery have been abolished over the years. Today stamped postcards, in their improved form, remain the only officially issued postal stationery that has remained efficient and in popular for over one hundred years. It is ironic, though, that before their introduction in Austria, a

An American postcard with paid reply.

**Letter cards from Bavaria (*top*),
France (*centre*) and Great Britain (*bottom*).**

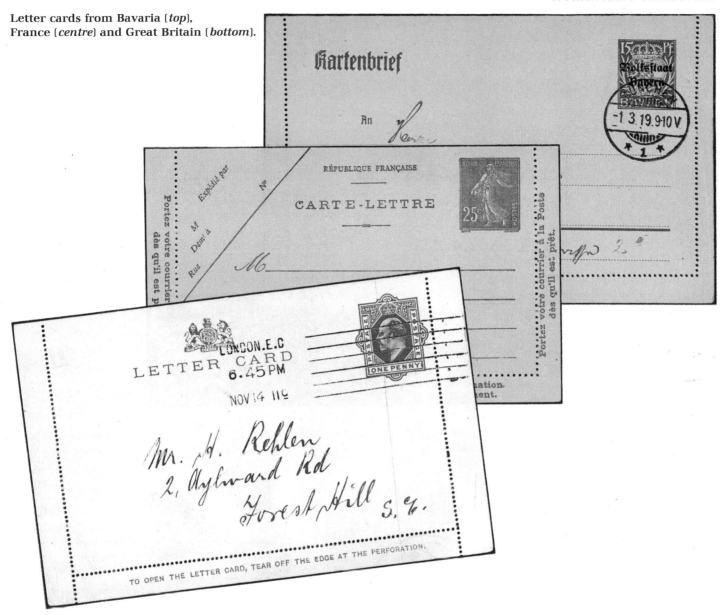

gress decreed that the address side should be divided into two parts by a vertical line. The right half was reserved for the address, while the sender could continue his message on the left side.

In addition to the ordinary stamped postcard, the so-called reply postcard was adopted; this consisted of a card folded over to form two postcards. For international use, the reply card was considered to be prepaid only if the recipient's answer was returned to the issuing country. If the foreign recipient decided to send his answer by express or recorded delivery, he had to pay an additional fee using the stamps of his own country. This explains why some answer portions of reply postcards bear the stamps of a foreign country.

The 1969 Tokyo Postal Union Congress finally abolished the use of reply cards in international communications because they hindered the sorting process and interfered with other automatic machinery. It was left to the discretion of individual postal administrations whether they would retain reply cards for domestic use.

Letter cards are another very common type of postal stationery. These are sheets of paper whose edges, about 10mm wide, are gummed and divided from the rest of the sheet by perforations. Once the message has been written, the letter card is folded over and sealed. The content of the letter card can only be read if the perforated edge is torn off.

The sheet serves as an envelope at the same time, and the address side bears an impressed stamp whose definitive value is the same as that of an ordinary letter. The first letter cards were issued in 1882 by France and Belgium. The Belgian, British and Swedish postal administrations still issue them.

Letter sheets differ from letter cards in that they are sheets or double sheets of paper that are folded into the shape of an envelope and gummed together using 10mm-wide overlapping edges. Although this type of postal stationery did not become popular in the 19th century, eventually it was revived in a special form — the aerogramme — after the Second World War.

The aerogramme is an international air letter with reduced postage. It was the British postal authorities that devised the air letter during the Second World War. During the War it was used for private correspondence to prisoners-of-war in Germany and Italy by airmail. The aerogramme would bear an inscription in English, German and French, for example, PRISONER-OF-WAR POST,

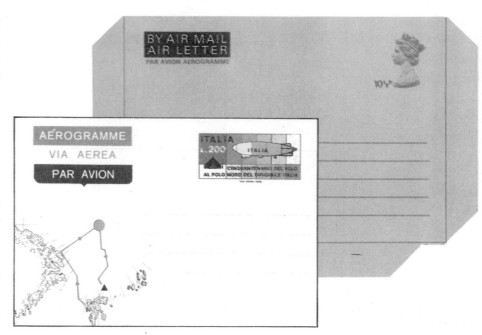

British and Italian aerogrammes.

KRIEGSGEFANGENENPOST, SERVICE DES PRISONNIERS DE GUERRE. After the War, aerogrammes were issued by other countries.

The aerogramme is a letter sheet made of thin but adequately durable paper, usually of a bluish-grey colour. The size of a folded aerogramme corresponds to that of a postcard, or slightly smaller. Its weight should not exceed five grams, and therefore it bears a warning that if the sender encloses another sheet of paper or any other item the aerogramme is liable to be conveyed

A British aerogramme from the Second World War, designed for private correspondence to prisoners-of-war.

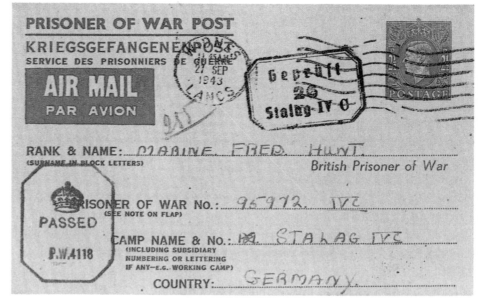

by land. In most countries, its postage rate is half the ordinary letter postage rate.

The aerogramme bears an inscription in French, which is the official language of the UPU. Occasionally it is also inscribed in the language of the issuing country. For instance, aerogrammes issued by the British post bear the inscription BY AIR MAIL/AIR LETTER/PAR AVION/AEROGRAMME.

Some countries issue aerogrammes without an impressed postage stamp, and therefore a stamp has to be affixed. Such a letter sheet is no longer considered to be an item of postal stationery, but becomes an ordinary letter paper instead.

Many aerogrammes have pictorial drawings, not only on the outside but inside as well. For example, British aerogrammes marking the 400th anniversary of William Shakespeare's birth were impressed with original stamps that were not part of the Jubilee stamp issue (also in 1964).

Aerogrammes have to be well differentiated from airmail envelopes, which, like the former, may bear characteristic slanted stripes. Some airmail envelopes appear with an impressed stamp, whose value corresponds to ten grams in weight. Airmail envelopes without an impressed stamp are on sale too.

Finally, wrappers for newspapers and magazines with an impressed stamp can be men-

A commemorative aerogramme issued in Great Britain to mark the Shakespeare Festival.

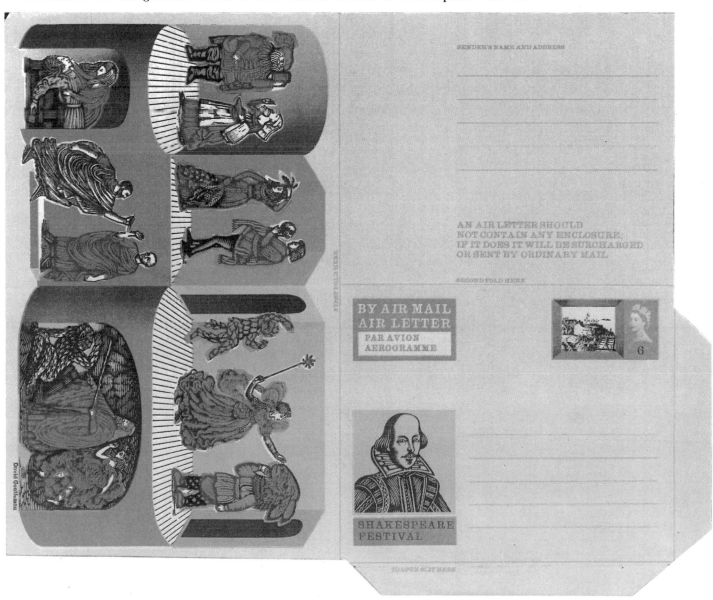

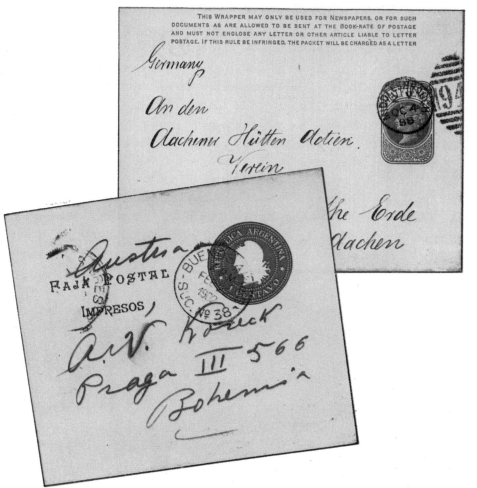

tioned here. These were issued for the first time in 1868 by the North German Postal Confederation, and were soon adopted by other countries. Some postal administrations, however, have never considered using them.

A number of postal administrations have issued other types of postal stationery, such as official envelopes, airmail postcards and parcel dispatch labels.

Newspaper wrappers used in Argentina and Great Britain.

8 *Special Kinds of Mail*

As we have seen so far, the historical development of the postal system is closely connected with the development of mankind. Postal administrations have always attempted to convey and deliver mail as quickly and as reliably as possible in order to respond to the needs of society. They have used a wide variety of transport methods that have left their mark in the form of special postmarks, official labels, inspectors' notes, and others. With time, all these items become of interest to philatelists.

Sea Mail

Although it is true that ships of all sorts carried mail for centuries, regular postal services only were established with the introduction of steam ships at the beginning of the 19th century.

While the use of the ships — whether oared or sailing vessels — for carrying mail has always been restricted to a certain degree, in some countries it has been the only means available. For instance, in the majority of the Chinese inland provinces, mail was always conveyed by postal vessels. Indian postal operations also were partly carried out on the rivers. The United States used river transport, in-

A post office on board ship, c. 1900.

cluding small vessels that could travel on tributaries that were inaccessible to large vessels. Similarly, in Europe sailing vessels provided an invaluable option. For example, the operation and maintenance of postal links between Great Britain and its northern and western inlands; along the Norwegian coastline; and with northern-most parts of tsarist Russia.

Sailing vessels were replaced by steamers at the beginning of the 19th century, which initially only transported mail. At one time, some ships, especially larger commercial steamboats, had postboxes that passengers would use to post mail on board ship. Later post offices were opened aboard ships, and postal clerks not only accompanied mail but also sorted it; this coincided with the appearance of the first ship letter-marks. The 1897 Washington Postal Union Congress decreed that all mail carried by ships that were not accompanied by post office clerks should be

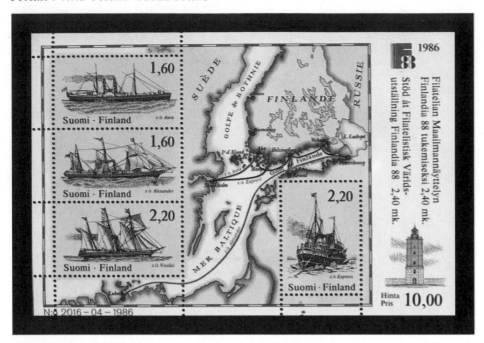

A commemorative miniature sheet depicting Finnish postal vessels from the mid-19th century.

Company stamp was of a rather high value — seventeen *kreuzer* — but in 1867 this was reduced to ten *kreuzer*. The stamps were not generally on sale; instead the port agent or the postal clerk on board would affix them to letters and cancel them immediately, which is why there were no post boxes on the vessels.

stamped with the word PAQUEBOT ('steamboat'). Today, the mail-carrying vessels that use distinctive postmarks do so to appeal to the tourists, who use these particular postal facilities.

The transport of overseas mail, especially in the northern Atlantic Ocean — from Germany, France, and Great Britain to and from the United States — was of primary significance. These postal links were developed towards the end of the 19th century, and only lost their importance with the widespread introduction of airmail services.

However, today mail can still be conveyed by sea, unless the sender opts for the much faster airmail transport, which of course involves an airmail surcharge. From a philatelist's point of view, today's mail carried by sea is uninteresting because it is often not designated in any particular way.

The activities of the First Imperial and Royal Privileged Danube Steamboat Company represent an interesting development in the history of river post. With the approval of the Austrian postal authorities, the Company also transported letters to and from the Danube ports in Serbia, Bulgaria, and Romania. In the beginning, letter transport was a private matter for the captains of individual vessels; a regular postal service was only introduced relatively recently in 1840.

At that time, river transport represented the technically most advanced and fastest means of transport. It is little wonder that the Company prospered and benefited from the carrying of letters. The only difficulty was a rather complex accounting system, because postage was collected in cash by ship's captains, port employees, and commercial agents as well. The issuing of the Company's own stamps from 1866 must have simplified this process, and must have resulted in even greater profits. The first

French and British ship letter marks (*above*). Illustrations of an additional stamp PAQUEBOT (*below*).

Steamboat inspectors ensured that no letter would be carried without an affixed stamp. If the inspector found stampless mail, the clerk responsible was liable to a heavy fine. The only exceptions were official letters transported on behalf of port and other authorities along the Danube, which were carried free of charge. However, they had to be dispatched by commercial agents, who would imprint them with an Ex-OFFICIO postmark, and their signature.

When a letter was carried along the Danube outside Austrian and Hungarian territories, only the Company stamp was needed. However, when the mail crossed the Austro-Hungarian border, additional postage in Austrian stamps was required. In 1880 the Company's postal services were terminated.

Submarine Post

Introduced during the First World War, submarine post is an unusual consequence of modern maritime post.

In 1916, Germany opened postal links with the United States, using the two commercial submarines 'Deutschland' and 'Bremen'. With the approval of the Reichspost, the German Insurance Bank of Berlin issued two commemorative stamp series: the first with nominative values ranging from five to fifty *marks*, the second ranging from five to one hundred *marks*.

The unusually high nominative value of the stamps was explained as being due to the combined postage and insurance premiums; the premiums were paid to the Bank, while the

Reichspost kept the postage. The stamps were issued in small numbers, and most of them — numbering around 500 specimens — went on sale.

Despite these huge charges, some letters were indeed carried by this special post. Arriving in New York, such a letter would be delivered by a special courier, or enclosed in a second envelope and conveyed by the ordinary

post. The breaking of diplomatic links between Germany and the United States in 1917 meant the end of this particular post.

Submarine post was revived before the Second World War. In 1938, the Spanish republic issued a series of six stamps and commemorative miniature sheet that bore pictures of the Republic's three submarines.

Stamp catalogues state that

Silistra, one of the Danube ports operating during the existence of the First Imperial and Royal Privileged Danube Steamboat Company.

The *Deutschland*, a German submarine. A copy of the painting in the German Postal History Archive, 1984.

these stamps were issued for a submarine post that operated during the time of the Spanish Civil War between Barcelona and Minorca. General Franco's troops, supported by Italian and German contingents — including the *Luftwaffe* Condor Squadron — were fighting the Republican government. They already occupied most of Spanish territory, while the Republican armies only held small areas around coastal towns. These could not be served by land, and the only available communication was by submarine link. Submarines transported supplies, ammunition, and mail to the coastal towns.

This submarine post was irregular and short-lived because the submarines had the entries to their home ports blockaded by enemy ships. The victory of Franco's insurgent armies terminated this peculiar service. On 31 March 1938 the Spanish Civil War ended, as did the validity of the stamps issued during the time of the Republic.

Railway Post

The first steam railway line was opened in 1822 at Hetton in England. The line was used to transport coal from the docks. It was followed in 1825 by the passenger service between Stockton and Darlington. The first French steam train appeared in 1823 on St Etienne-Andrézieux line. The United States opened its first railway line between Baltimore and Ellicotts-Mills in 1829. And in 1835 Belgium introduced this new form of transport, and Germany started to operate the Fürth-Nürnberg line. Gradually the rail network spread to other countries.

The idea of sorting mail *en route* appeared first in England, which can be considered the cradle of both railways and railway post. The first rail post office was run on a trial basis in January 1830 in the London-Birmingham line. It was such a success, that when in December of the same year a regular passenger service was introduced on this route, night and day mail services were

A German submarine postmark, used on all mail destined for a voyage early in 1917 which was subsequently cancelled because of the political situation.

A letter sent by the Spanish submarine post from Mahón on the island of Minorca.

A series of stamps issued to commemorate the 150th anniversary of the Liverpool-Manchester railway line.

The opening of the Fürth-Nürnberg railway line on 7 December 1835.

put into operation. Postal clerks worked in a special railway carriage, which became a travelling post office. They sorted the mail according to individual destinations, postmarking it and handing it over to local posts. The establishment of the first travelling post offices resulted in simpler and cheaper postal operations.

Philatelists are principally interested in the mail that is posted directly from the railway platform into postboxes set into the sides of mail trains. Only these items would get a special postmark. Even a railway parcel label would be of interest in the case of registered mail.

In the beginning, all letters transported and processed by the travelling post offices were postmarked on their reverse side. These postmarks usually bore the names of principal towns on the route of which the travelling post office (TPO) operated. On the return journey, the order of the towns would be reversed. In France, the direction was sometimes indicated using the words T for *tour* or outward journey, and R, for *retour*, return journey. In recent years this rail post has been severely restricted, and replaced by air and road services. In some countries rail

posts have been abolished completely. Thus collecting railway postmarks is rather difficult because of their scarcity and lack of detailed cataloguing.

One postal peculiarity can be mentioned here: in the second half of the 19th century, a TPO operated on a route close to the Danube estuary on the Black Sea. It issued its own railway stamps. Several years prior to the establishment of this TPO, a Romanian duchy ruled by the Turks had been founded there. However,

the railway stamps do not usually bear the name of the stamp-issuing country, the Romanian duchy of Turkey; instead they bear the initials DBSR, and the inscriptions LOCAL POST, KÜS-TENDJE & CZERNA WODA. The DBSR stands for the name of an English company — the Danube and Black Sea Railway — which had constructed the railway line between the towns of Küstendje, present-day Constanta, and the important Danube port of Czerna Woda on the lower reaches of the

The TPO wagon used on the Paris-Lyon railway line *c.* 1910.

The railway stamp only would be affixed to those letters that the company actually collected from the sender. The majority of letters, however, were tranported in sealed bags on this route.

Pneumatic Posts

Pneumatic posts were established in many cities in the second half of the 19th century. They consisted of a system of underground tubes that connected a main office, usually situated within the general post office (GPO) with major city post offices. Mail was enclosed in steel or aluminium cylinders of different sizes. Each cylinder could carry a certain number of telegrams as well as postcards and letters. The cylinders were propelled through fifty to seventy millimetre-diameter tubes using a front vacuum, and increased rear air pressure created in the

river. The company transported goods, passengers, and letters from several other southern European countries. In fact, this was a local post operating with the consent of Turkey and Romania.

Railway postmarks (*from top to bottom*): Austria, Bavaria, and France.

Right: A letter transported by the Austrian Rail Post.

engine room through a system of furnaces, pumps, and valves. Cylinders could be dispatched at a speed of one kilometre per minute.

The first pneumatic lines usually connected the main telegraph office with the stock exchange.

Pneumatic posts adopted the slogan 'Time is Money', and concentrated on the speedy dispatch of telegrams to individual city post offices. These would arrange for the subsequent fast delivery of telegrams.

The first pneumatic post was established throughout London in 1862, to be followed by Berlin in 1865, Paris in 1866/7, Vienna in 1875, Prague around 1900. Marseilles, and Italian, American, and other cities also created similar services. By 1893 eight more British towns adopted the pneumatic system, but used it for official purposes only.

Over the years, the pneumatic system was improved, and the number of participating offices extended. The principal function was not only telegram delivery from individual post offices to the city GPO, which had postal links to other towns, but in the opposite direction as well, which shortened the time needed to deliver a telegram. The pneumatic post would also send express delivery letters and postcards, and, later, air mail letters as well, to and from post offices responsible for their further delivery.

All of these are examples of using pneumatic posts for official purposes. In some cities, however, private correspondence also was conveyed by this means. Special stationery — envelopes and postcards with an impressed stamp — would be issued. The Italian post office even introduced special postage stamps. Today philatelists collect items carried by pneumatic systems because of their relative scarcity.

The beginnings of pneumatic posts in Paris (*above*) and Philadelphia (*below*).

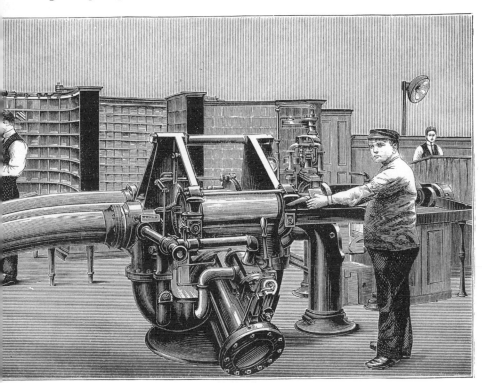

Since the Second World War, the development of telephone and telex systems has resulted in far fewer telegrams being sent. Telephones have gradually replaced the private mail sent by pneumatic post, which has led to the abolition of pneumatic services for the public, although they are still used for official postal purposes.

Disinfected Mail

Disinfected mail includes the earliest postal items, primarily dating from the pre-stamp period, which were sent from territories ravaged by plague and cholera epidemics.

From the historical point of view, it is possible to divide these quarantined letters (letters on which a period of isolation was imposed) into pre-1830 items, which usually come from the plague-infested territories, and post-1830 items, coming from the cholera-ravaged areas. These letters were disinfected not only when they were carried from one country to another, such as from Prussia to Austria, but also within a country, and among individual towns.

The earliest quarantined mail dates from the 16th century, but evidence of disinfection can only be traced from the end of the 18th century, the letters of which bear handwritten notes, postmarks, seals, or labels. The notes were inscribed in various languages, and often given in an abbreviated form, such as SANITAETES SAN., DESINFIZIERT, STELISIERT, NETTA FUORI ET DETTO ('Clean inside and outside'). At first, only external disinfection was carried out, but later the contents were also disinfected by sprinkling the mail with vinegar, and subsequently by fumigating it in sulphur fumes or formaldehyde.

Disinfection procedures differed at individual ports, borders, and towns. In general, however, all goods, mail, and persons were handled by quarantine stations. People were kept in isolation for a number of days; goods and mail were disinfected. Some quarantine stations operated for a short period only, and the letters handled by them are rare. Each station operated its own system of disinfection, and used various methods to provide evidence of this. Thus, several thousand varieties of hand stamps and seals for this purpose are known to have existed.

Regulations for disinfecting mail in the 17th and 18th centuries are well documented. Those traditional protective postal regulations were updated in 1831, when Europe was struck by a great cholera epidemic. The German regulations of that time decree that all letters conveyed from a region or a country where cholera outbreaks had been confirmed 'should be fumigated for the purpose of their disinfection'. This was done in several ways: the letters were pierced by a special needle resembling a shoemaker's awl; in very suspicious cases the letter then was slit at one side, and only then inserted in a fumigating device where it was subjected to high temperatures, vinegar vapour and sulphur, and formaldehyde fumes. Later, larger quarantine stations that handled mail in bulk began to use special tools in order to pierce their letters.

It is evident today that all of these measures must have had a certain psychological impact on the public — reassuring them and making them less frightened of the spread of disease — but they cannot possibly have resulted in a proper and efficient disinfection process.

The disinfected letters that have been exposed to such drastic measures do not look very appealing. However, they are of historic value, as they are the only remaining witnesses to the postal system operated during the period of contagious cholera and plague epidemics of the 18th and 19th centuries.

The last major disinfection of mail was carried out by the Aus-

Cylinders used to deliver pneumatic mail in Berlin, London, Philadelphia, New York, and Boston at the end of the 19th century.

An Austrian postcard for the Prague pneumatic post (*right*)

A Czechoslovak postcard for pneumatic post (*below*).

A French postcard for the Paris pneumatic post (*above*).

An Italian postage stamp for pneumatic post (*below*).

trian army during the First World War. Special quarantine letters do still occur. For instance, research institutes exchange letters throughout the world in which seeds are enclosed, and such letters have to be disinfected.

Field and Military Mail

In ancient times, messages carried by couriers principally concerned governmental or military affairs. Those who conveyed army commanders' dispatches could be referred to as military couriers. In the Middle Ages, military messages were carried in a similar fashion, but in the late Middle Ages, couriers used existing postal links. During military campaigns, however, it was necessary to have alternative postal links. Written evidence shows that one of the earliest special courier links was established in 1496 during the Italian military campaign of the Emperor Maximilian I (1493–1519). Later, postal arrangements during individual military campaigns were referred to as 'field posts', and were headed by an army postmaster, whose duty it was to operate and supervise a courier service. Military courier links did not have a strict organizational structure, and couriers were only dispatched when required.

At the beginning of the 19th century, it became evident that military courier services could not satisfy the ever-growing need for the transport of official and private correspondence. Therefore, field post offices were set up during military campaigns. The field post was a well-organized service that arranged for the transport of mail between soldiers and the Front, and also among troops and their families

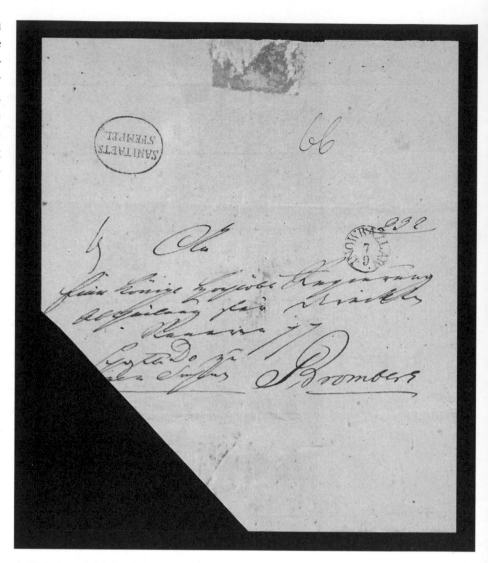

A disinfected letter from the latter half of 1831. One of its corners was cut off to facilitate disinfection.

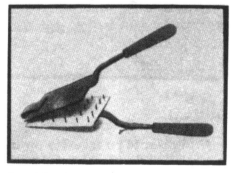

Special pincers to pierce mail that had to be disinfected.

and military authorities at home. The field post office reached its peak during the First World War when it provided a service for tens of millions of people.

The fact that field post was censored is documented by censor marks and even censors' notes. During the First and Second World Wars soldiers were obliged to use field postcards, which speeded up the work of the censors because they were not delayed by having to open letters. This military mail was carried free of charge, which ex-

plains why no stamps were affixed to it.

Prisoner-of-War Posts

The war that started in Europe in 1914 soon turned into a world war. Millions of men were mobilized and joined the warring armies. Hundreds of soldiers' families waited anxiously for news from the Fronts. Field posts carried hundreds of thousands of field postcards, which testified to the recipients that the senders had been alive and well when writing. Any delay or interruption in postal communication meant that hundreds of families could be worrying whether a father or a son was still alive or not.

For many, it came as a huge relief to receive mail from a prisoner-of-war camp situated somewhere within enemy territory. According to international law, such mail was exempt from postage, and was exchanged among the combatant countries by the Red Cross, which also organized the search for soldiers reported as missing in action.

Important documentary philatelic material has been saved from the Second World War, namely postal consignments, letters, and postcards. These bear witness to the fate of many members of the Resistance, as mail from prisons, and labour and concentration camps established by the Nazis can be found among these.

Captured Polish officers were detained in special camps where they were permitted to organize their own internal postal service and issue their own postage stamps. In this case, at least, the Nazis observed the Geneva Conventions regarding prisoners-of-war, allowing imprisoned officers to administer their own camps; they were also given pocket-money calculated according to rank. One of their biggest achievements, the organization of an internal postal service, provided an invaluable service for the interned officers, even if it did not have any official links with the outside world. In several instances this internal postal service helped to improve communication with the camp commandants.

From 1942 onwards, camp postal services gradually began to issue their own postage stamps. These stamps were primitively printed as single specimens on wastepaper or even on the edges of old German newspapers, using wooden blocks. In 1944, when the Olympic Games would have been held had it not been for the War, two Polish prisoner-of-war camps produced a stamp with five Olympic circles, and another stamp bearing the inscription OLYMPIADA. They were the only stamp issuers who that year symbolically expressed their wish for an end to the War. By issuing the Olympic stamps the prisoners recalled the fact that the Ancient Greeks had interrupted all of their wars and military campaigns for the duration of the Games, which were at the time considered to be sacred.

Polar Posts

At the beginning of the 20th century, post offices were even

DEL'ARMEE·DIT.

The first-known field postmark used by French troops during the 1688–1697 Italian military campaign. The postmark was found on a letter dating from 1696.

A French field post office during the First World War.

A letter carried by the Austrian field post in 1855 during the Russian-Turkish War when Moldavia and Wallachia were occupied by Austrian troops.

established outside territories permanently inhabited by mankind: in the Arctic and Antarctic regions. Due to the preparations for the 1957–1958 International Geophysical Year, many more permanent polar stations at the North and South Poles were established. As more and more mail was dispatched from these remote and inaccessible regions, philatelists became interested, marking the beginning of so-called 'Polar philately'.

It is rather difficult to acquire mail that has been struck with postmarks of Polar stations that are established on ice-caps floating in the Arctic Ocean, or on the icy islands of Antarctica, the southernmost continent. As well, the reliability and regularity of written links between Polar explorers and the rest of the world is subject to the vagaries of weather conditions.

Some people today say that Polar post is old-fashioned and should make way for telecommunication links. However, although such methods are widely used, Polar researchers still require postal services. Richard E. Byrd (1888—1957), the famous American Polar explorer, wrote years ago that without doubt radio had been an important invention, but the post had indeed been a miracle. The Polar explorer will always consider a letter

Sending letters through a field post at the end of the 19th century.

from home to be the most welcome message of all.

Mail from the famous Norwegian explorer Roald Amundsen's expedition (1918—1924) is significant in Polar postal history. Amundsen (1872—1928) was the first explorer to reach the South Pole in 1911. He also successfully completed several voyages across the Arctic Ocean, but one expedition, on the sailing ship 'Maud', was especially important.

Amundsen set sail on 18 June 1918 to explore the northern coasts of Europe and Asia. When he realized that the 'Maud' would not be able to circumnavigate the Taymyr peninsula because of bad weather, he decided to winter over in the shelter of the Chelyuskin peninsula. However, he sent two of his crew with mail to Dickson Island, a distance of 900 kilometres, where there was a Polar station. One sailor died of exhaustion as they neared their journey's end. His companion struggled on, and when nearly exhausted hid a bag of mail, perhaps hoping that he might collect it later. He in turn perished two kilometres from the Polar station. The mail bag only was dis-

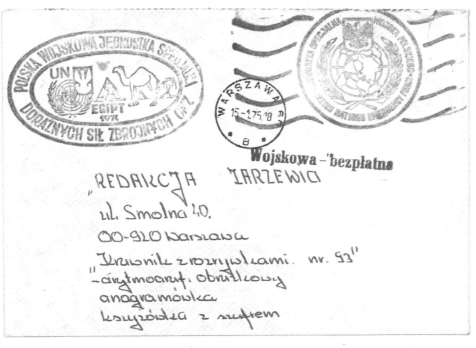

An Austrian field post censor's mark from the First World War.

Above, from top to bottom: A letter delivered in England during the Second World War by Czechoslovak field post; a French field postcard from the First World War, returned to the sender because the delivery was impossible; a 1974 letter sent from a Polish military unit serving as part of the UN peace-keeping forces in Egypt.

covered several years later; all of Amundsen's letters were found to be intact.

Amundsen's 1918—1924 expedition bequeathed one other treat to philatelists: postcards that had been on board the 'Maud' and had wintered over on the Chelyuskin peninsula bear two postmarks depicting a sailing vessel, and are inscribed with POLHAVET, which translates as 'an ocean by the Pole'. They also bear the date and the geographical co-ordinates that stand for the name of a post office.

Some collectors maintain that these postcards are related to a voyage that Amundsen had intended to undertake on the ship 'Fram'. This is supported by the fact that the postcard's address side bears an inscription in four languages on the left-hand side stating that the postcard had been carried aboard the 'Fram' across the Arctic Ocean, and then posted to the recipient. A facsimile of Amundsen's signature is placed under the inscription. The reverse of the postcard depicts the 'Fram', which was the expedition ship of Fridtjof Nansen (1861–1930), another Norwegian Arctic explorer.

Amundsen originally had intended to use the old three-masted sailing ship 'Fram', and had the postcards printed in order to assist in the financing of his expedition. However, the First World War intervened, and he had to

Above: A postcard sent from a prisoner-of-war camp in India to Austria in 1917. The sender had to use the pre-printed text; unwanted sentences were crossed out. The sender was only allowed to add the date and his signature, or the postcard would not be delivered.

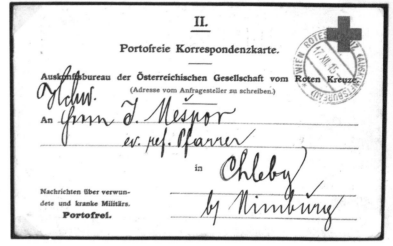

An Austrian Red Cross postcard from the First World War with notification of a soldier reported as missing in action (*above*).

A postcard of a Unit searching for missing Germans in the Soviet Occupation Zone from the period after the Second World War (*below*).

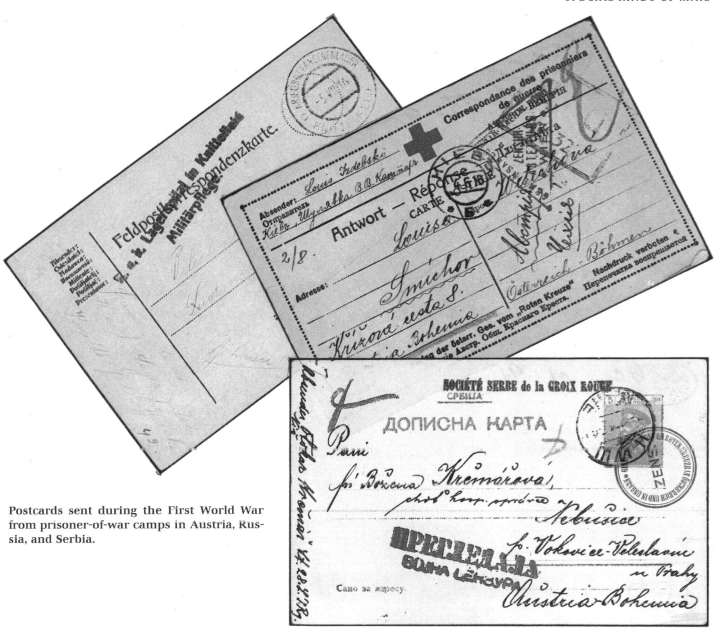

Postcards sent during the First World War from prisoner-of-war camps in Austria, Russia, and Serbia.

A letter sent during the First World War from a prisoner-of-war camp in Great Britain.

A letter from the Nazi concentration camp for women at Ravensbrück.

A scientific polar station in the Arctic.

A miniature sheet, 'The North Pole Floating Station', was issued in 1958 by the Soviet postal authorities. The former Soviet Union gradually established more than twenty floating scientific stations, all called 'North Pole'. This illustrated miniature sheet was first used for postal purposes on 'North Pole-6'. This station began its research work north of Wrangel Island in April 1957. It was sited on a floating ice-cap 14 km long, 11 km wide and 9—12 km thick. The station completed its mission in September 1959 when the currents carried the ice-cap into the Gronsky Sea, and any further stay on it would have become dangerous.

postpone the start of his voyage. Amundsen then decided that the 'Fram' would soon become outmoded, and had a new ship built according to his own design. He named the new sailing ship 'Maud'. In February 1926 the postcards depicting and referring to the 'Fram' were delivered to the recipients, but they had been transported to the Arctic by the 'Maud'. Only a few postcards printed shortly before Amundsen set sail give the correct name of the expedition's ship, 'Maud'.

The attention of philatelists to Polar post entires was increased by the 1931 joint venture of the German airship 'Graf Zeppelin' LZ 127 and the Soviet ice-breaker 'Malygin'. The airship and the ice-breaker joined forces in an extensive programme of Arctic research that was marked by the issue of German and Soviet commemorative stamps. The 'Graf Zeppelin' and the 'Malygin' were each equipped with a post office, which used special postmarks.

The 'Graf Zeppelin' began its Polar expedition from Friedrichshafen on 24 July 1931. The 'Malygin' set sail from Archangel on 18 July 1931 and met the 'Graf Zeppelin' in Pacific Bay of Franz Josef Land. The airship landed by the Bay and mail was exchanged: the 'Graf Zeppelin' was carrying 50,000 postal items weighing a total of 300 kilograms, while the 'Malygin' handed over mail weighing 120 kilograms.

Polar post history is extensive, but if nothing else the ice-cap stations named 'North Pole' deserve a mention. The first of them, 'North Pole-I', was manned by Soviet Polar explorers, who were taken by air to an ice-cap. In the 274 days they spent there, the

A postcard sent from the Spitsbergen Islands, belonging to Norway, situated within the Arctic Sea. The postcard was transported by Amundsen's ship 'Maud'.

A postmark used on the 'Maud', which uses geographical co-ordinates in place of a named post office.

into sectors belonging to the former Soviet Union, the United States, Canada, Denmark, and Norway. Philatelic material arriving from each sector will undoubtedly keep philatelists interested for years to come.

Polar post has a rich history in Antarctica too. The first mention of an official postmark is that of an Argentinian station dating from 1904. Only in the last thirty years, however, have more Antarctic stations been established. For instance, the first Soviet postmark was struck at the Mirny Station – which became the main Soviet expeditionary base — in 1956. The expedition's leader also had at his disposal a handstamp of the Mirny post office.

By 1959, twelve countries had established their own permanent research stations in the Antarctic

A letter sent from the Soviet floating station 'North Pole-22'.

ice-cap travelled over 2,000 kilometres before the explorers were evacuated by the ice-breakers 'Taymyr' and 'Murmansk'. The explorers accumulated valuable data, and proved that it was possible to live and work on a floating ice-cap for a prolonged period of time. However, a post office only was established on 'North Pole-4'; this started operating in April 1954. This post office used its own postmark inscribed with 'North Pole-4'; from that time onwards Polar stations 'North Pole-5' to '22' postmarked their correspondence as well.

The Arctic is divided politically

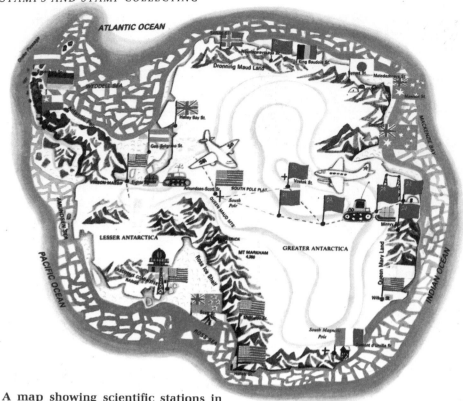

A map showing scientific stations in Antarctica (in the 1980s).

ance of entires that make it possible for philatelists to document the work of individual scientific expeditions in those distant parts of the world. The entires bear Polar-station postmarks, and additional postmarks of each respective expedition. They have the charm and romantic appeal of remote lands, which most collectors may never be fortunate enough to visit.

Registered Mail

Registered mail is not a modern postal innovation: it has existed for over 300 years. Formerly, when messages were delivered by couriers, every letter in fact was registered because detailed records were kept of each dispatch and delivery. It was only in the 17th century that some postal items received preferential treatment, and were handled with special care. This is well documented in postal regulations such as the 1677 'Postal Regulations of the Elector Johann George II von Sachsen', and in the 1695 'Austrian Postal Regula-

region during the preparatory and major work carried out in the Third Geophysical Year.

In contrast to the Arctic, there are some disputed territories in Antarctica. Several countries may raise claims to one territory, and therefore even the establishment of post offices is of political

significance, stressing territorial rights. Leaders of individual expeditions are appointed postmasters and are equipped beforehand with hand stamps and postage stamps.

The establishment of postal facilities in the Arctic and Antarctic regions have led to the appear-

A commemorative postmark from a philatelic exhibition 'Norvex 80' marking The Day of Polar Philately.

An Austrian pre-stamp registered letter (*right*).

A registered letter in a special envelope issued for Kenya, Uganda, and Tanganyika sent to London during the Second World War.

tions of Leopold I'. Nevertheless, it was some time before formal arrangements for the handling of registered mail were introduced.

It was customary in the 18th century for two types of postal items to be carried: routine mail, and special mail — which the sender wished to be handled preferentially, and delivered to a specified address. Such letters were entered into the registration book at a post office, and the sender was given a special receipt, or the so-called 'certificate of posting'.

Every letter was endorsed with a serial number corresponding to that on the certificate of posting, and also visibly marked to identify its importance. In Austria, registered letters were marked with the inscription NB (from the Latin *nota bene*, 'note it well') in red or brown wax; later, dark ink was used. After a time, the abbreviation NB was replaced by a written sign consisting of a number of vertical or slanted lines, which were crossed by one or more horizontal lines.

Inscriptions and postmarks incorporating such words as REGISTERED, RECOMMANDIRT, RACCOMANDATO, already appear on most registered mail towards the end of the pre-stamp period.

In the 1870s, post offices in Alsace-Lorraine began to use special registration labels on a trial basis. Once these had proved their worth, their use spread to other German states. Great Britain introduced special envelopes with an impressed stamp (postal stationery), which bore the distinctly printed word REGISTERED on its address side for use with registered mail.

Examples of registration labels (*right, from top to bottom*): London (Great Britain), Rotterdam (the Netherlands), Hamburg (Germany), USA, Addis Ababa (Ethiopia), Mecca (Saudi Arabia), Hong Kong, Tel Aviv-Yafo (Israel), Athens (Greece), Alexandria (Egypt), Ecuador.

Special registration labels used during world philatelic exhibitions (*from left to right*): 'WIPA 1965' (Austria), 'Hafnia '87' (Denmark), 'Bulgaria '89' (Bulgaria), 'Praga '88' (Czechoslovakia).

Postage stamps for registered letters (*from top to bottom*): US, Canada, Columbia.

From 1 January 1883, the Paris Postal Union Congress decreed that all registration postmarks and existing registration labels should bear the initial R. The letter R still identifies registered mail in all member states of the Universal Postal Union.

Postal administrations in individual countries have gradually adopted registration labels for registered mail. Labels are at present also used for special events, such as major philatelic exhibitions. Along with the routine information, they bear the name of the exhibition.

In addition to registration labels, some countries such as the former Soviet Union, Spain, and the United States use hand stamps incorporating all the details of the registration label, leaving the serial number of a registered postal item to be filled in by hand. Those countries that do not use Latin characters may use different labels for postage abroad; the text will be inscribed in Latin characters, while for example, the labels will be written in Cyrillic for domestic use.

Labels for insured letters, introduced in the 1920s, are fairly similar to registration labels. Instead of the letter R they are inscribed with the letter V (from the French word *valeur,* 'value'), which usually is printed in black on a red background.

Express Mail

In the second half of the 19th century, express services were introduced in many countries. The 1860s Pony Express represents an interesting chapter in the history of express postal services.

The Pony Express was established to maintain and provide a fast and efficient postal service across the United States: from the Mississippi to the Pacific Ocean through Kansas, Nebraska, Wyoming, Utah, Nevada, and California. These routes were carefully reconnoitred, and fortified relay stations were established every twenty kilometres. These halts were equipped with relays of ponies and food supplies, and were protected by armed guards.

Examples of labels for insured letters: Kladno (Bohemia, *above*), Frankfurt-am-Main (Germany, *below*).

A recruitment poster for the Pony Express.

Frontiersmen, backwoodsmen and early settlers set out on their journey west, confiscating and claiming land from the Indians. Distances between individual settlements were vast, and the isolation was extremely threatening. Horses were the only fast means of transport.

When the Pony Express recruited riders, it did not try to conceal from them the dangers involved. Posters and leaflets openly advertised for 'young, skinny, wiry fellows not over 18. Must be expert riders, willing to risk death daily. Orphans preferred. Wages $25.00 per week.' Every new employee was obliged to undergo a strict medical check-up, and when signing his contract he also had to take an oath along the following lines: 'I shall not drink or swear, and always behave honestly, so help me God.'

The Company soon hired 100 volunteers and bought 300 ponies, which were assigned to indi-vidual relay stations. The Pony Express carried mail from St Joseph, Missouri, to Sacramento, California. The rider would carry mail in a canvas saddle bag; he would be lightly armed and have a supply of biscuits, bacon, and a flagon of tea. To announce his arrival at a relay station he would blow a horn. The station in turn would prepare for his speedy departure. The exchange of ponies lasted a mere one minute and ten seconds, a speed calculated by the Company, although the riders themselves were always attempting to set new records.

The journey that the Express riders had to make was unsafe because a lone rider was often the prey of Indian tribes. These attacks were so common, that the Company turned to the government and asked for military protection. However negotiations were prolonged, and meanwhile the Company's financial losses grew greater. Finally the Pony Ex-press was forced to discontinue its service and to dismiss all of its employees. In June 1865 the service resumed and ran for some time, but it could not satisfy the increasing demand for postal items to be carried, and was replaced by stage-coaches.

In the latter half of the 19th century the transport of mail was speeded by the establishment of new post offices; the introduction of stage-coaches, relay postal services, and primarily, by rail links. However, despite these varied means of transport, the time that elapsed between the arrival of post and its sorting and delivery remained practically unchanged. This was especially true in those places where mail was delivered once a day. Letters and other messages intended to reach their recipients quickly would often, therefore, be left at the post office until the following day.

In order to limit such delays, express letters were introduced,

The Pony Express Route from St Joseph to California, and the Butterfield Stage Line, one of the famous stage coach routes.

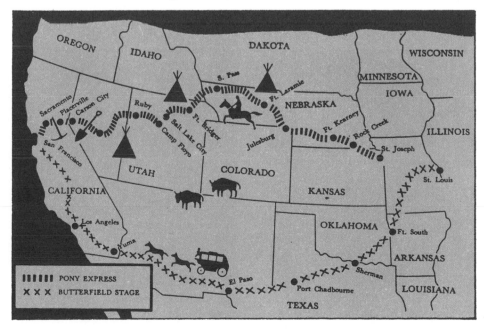

A Pony Express rider.

which were carried by a special messenger directly to the recipient. At first, express letters were delivered with no regard for the time of the day or night. The night delivery was, understandably, not very popular with the public, as shown by handwritten notes on contemporary letters, such as 'Express, No Night Delivery.' This, in turn, led to restricted night delivery services.

At present, if a sender wishes to have his postal item delivered as speedily as possible after handing it in at the mailing post office, he can inscribe it with the note EXPRESS on the address side, and pay an additional fee for such an express delivery service.

A Spanish express delivery letter franked with a meter postage stamp.

Left: Examples of express delivery labels (*from top to bottom*) — Austria, Italy, Switzerland, Turkey, Bulgaria, the Netherlands, Great Britain, Finland, Czechoslovakia, Luxembourg.

In some countries, the sender may, in domestic services, add the words NIGHT ALSO if the item is to be delivered between 22.00 and 06.00 hours.

Stamp-Dispensing Machines

For years a number of countries have used stamp-dispensing machines that sell stamps of the most common denominations when a specific number of coins is inserted. These machines sell either books of stamps, or coils of stamps.

Coil stamps, distributed in 500 or 1,000 stamp rolls, not in sheets, are designed only for use in automatic slot machines. They are perforated either on two opposite sides or on all four sides. Books of stamps consist of one or several sheets of stamps of the most common denominations, enclosed in covers. They may

Examples of books of stamps: France (*above*), Germany and Sweden (*below*). They are interesting for collectors because they may combine stamps of different nominal values, or the stamps may be perforated on two or three sides only.

Postage stamps issued in stamp rolls.

also be dispensed from automatic machines.

In 1976, Switzerland introduced a new type of slot machine that dispenses meter-franked stamps. These automatic machines do not contain ready-printed postal stationery, but rolls of phosphorescent gummed paper with a light-grey network that contains violet threads. The customer selects the required postal denomination, which may range from 00.05 to 99.95 Swiss francs. He or she inserts the appropriate coinage, and the machine issues stationery with the value imprinted in red. Its function is the same as that of the stamps, that is, to prepay postage by affixing it to the postal item.

The advantage of these modern slot machines compared to coil stamps and books of stamps is that they provide the customer with meter stamps of a chosen value at any time. They have now been adopted in other countries, such as Great Britain, France, Finland, and Hong Kong.

9 Aerophilately

Pigeon posts in the Middle Ages.

Aerophilately is a branch of philately that deals with the collecting and study of airmail stamps and philatelic material connected with airmail transport. It includes pigeon posts, balloon posts, and aircraft posts.

Pigeon Posts

The first messengers used by mankind to tranport messages by air were carrier pigeons. Written records have been preserved that document that pigeon posts existed in Ancient Egypt, Greece, and Rome. The Ancient Egyptians took carrier pigeons on board their ships, and would dispatch them homeward with messages describing the voyage. The Roman writer Gaius Plinius Secundus, the Elder (AD 23–79) mentions in his 'Natural History' (*Historia Naturalis*) that Decimus Brutus had used carrier pigeons to transmit messages in 43 BC from Mutina (present-day Modena), which had been besieged by Marcus Antonius. In Greece, carrier pigeons were dispatched throughout the country during the Olympic Games to announce the Olympic winners. The Chinese also used carrier pigeons for transmitting messages rapidly; these were occasional 'flights' only, as no records have been preserved to show that a regular pigeon post was ever established at that time.

It was in the mid-15th century that a Turkish sultan established a regular pigeon post service between Constantinople and Budapest. In the first half of the 19th century a similar regular service operated between the big banking houses of Paris, London, Antwerp, and Frankfurt. The pigeons would transport messages concerning exchange rates and other financial matters.

A famous pigeon service was set up during the siege of Paris during the Franco-Prussian War (1870–1871). Initially the pigeon service was used for official correspondence, which was copied, first manually and later photographically, on to thin paper. Soon this service was extended to the public as well; mail from the whole of France was collect-

A carrier pigeon.

ed at Tours to be conveyed to Paris by the pigeon post.

The famous French photographer René Dagron (1819–1900) invented a method of reducing messages photographically, which in turn increased the number of items carried by the pigeon post. Messages were arranged in columns, and printed in tiny print on huge sheets of paper. These sheets were placed on panels and photographed on a roll of film 35×65 mm. A single pigeon could carry up to eighteen rolls of film at a time. On arrival in Paris, the messages were projected on to a screen, copied, and then sent on to the recipients.

Because Dagron did not have ideal conditions for his photography at Tours, compared to his well-equipped studio in Paris, the film negatives had technical flaws, with up to seventy percent being of substandard quality. The pigeon often had to carry messages several times before the Paris postal authorities acknowledged their receipt.

The service was highly profitable for the French post office as it charged half a franc per word. A single trip brought in a 35,000 franc profit to the post office. The pigeon post service was abandoned eventually, but during its existence, it had been successful in transmitting over 60,000 airborne messages.

Towards the end of the 19th century, a private pigeon post was established to maintain regular communications between Great Barrier Island and the city of Auckland in New Zealand. At that time the Island was filled with gold prospectors and lumberjacks. As mail was transported to the Island only twice

a month, one Walter Fricker decided to set up a pigeon post in 1896. The pigeons carried short letters written on silk paper, which were tied around their necks or feet, or placed under their wings. Initially the pigeons were taken in both directions by ship. Later, Fricker managed to arrange for a two-way pigeon service that delivered mail daily. There are conflicting reports as to when this service was abandoned. Some say it was discontinued only when the government telegraph service was established in 1908, while others argue that it lasted for only a few months because it was hugely unprofitable.

From that time onwards the pigeons were used rarely. However, the German army established special pigeon post units during the First World War. Their mail bears a special postmark, that is, KGL. PREUSS. BRIEF-TUBEN-SCHLAG ('Royal Prussian Dovecote'),

and is greatly coveted by most collectors. Since 1945 pigeon posts have been used to promote publicity for philatelic exhibitions.

Balloon Posts

One of the first attempts to carry mail by balloon took place in July 1859. A balloon called 'Jupiter' was launched from La Fayette, Indiana, carrying a bag of mail. For years after it was presumed that none of the transported mail survived, but then a letter was discovered in 1957. The United States issued a commemorative stamp to mark this historic event in 1959.

Balloon services, which were combined with the pigeon post, maintained communications with Paris during the Franco-Prussian War, and represent one of the most famous chapters in the history of ballooning. Led by the outstanding photographer, cartoonist, and craftsman, Nadar, whose

A 'pigeongram' — a message carried by pigeon on the occasion of a postage stamp exhibition.

Balloon launches always captured public attention.

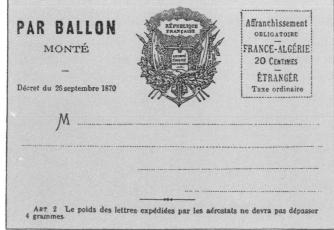

A postcard for the French balloon post dispatched from Paris besieged by Prussian troops using a manned balloon.

real name was Félix Tournachon (1820—1910), Parisian balloonists volunteered their help in the very first days of the siege in September 1870. They met the chief of the Paris GPO and discussed the establishment and operation of air postal links between the embattled city and the French government, which had by then moved to Tours, and later to Bordeaux. There were balloons in Paris at that time. Deserted railway stations were turned into workshops that manufactured new balloons and were supervised by experienced balloonists.

The first flight, which was extremely dangerous and risky, took place on 23 September 1870. An old balloon called 'Neptune' flew over Versailles and landed near Evreux. The balloon carried a vast quantity of official documents and private correspondence written on thin 'airmail' paper. The second balloon, which took off from Paris, also transported several pigeons, belonging to the best Parisian pigeon-breeders.

The balloon post transported letters, postal cards, and newspapers out of Paris. Newspapers were accepted for transport only if they were printed on thin paper; some were tied by a newspaper wrapper, while others were enclosed in an envelope. Letter-card postage was ten *centimes*; postage for a letter weighing up to four grams was twenty *centimes*. Heavier letters were excluded from this service.

The links between Paris and the outside were well organized. Every flight out of Paris, however, meant there were fewer experienced balloonists left who were capable of navigating balloons, as

Projecting photographic messages, which were brought to Paris by carrier pigeons.

they could not of course return to the besieged city. It was necessary to train new balloonists from among military and civilian volunteers.

Despite the fact that to maintain regular communications balloons were built rapidly and launched in poor weather conditions, there were surprisingly few accidents. Between 23 September 1870 and 28 January 1871 sixtyseven balloons were launched: of these, fifty-five transported mail bags; five balloons with their crews were captured by the Prussians, and only two went missing and were presumably lost at sea. This meant that most of the correspondence reached its intended destination. In the autumn of 1873 the wreckage of an unmanned ballon was discovered in southern Africa. In addition to manned balloons (*ballons montés*), small unmanned balloons (*ballons libres*) were launched.

The balloons even transported some important personalities and wealthy citizens who could afford the high transport charges. The most famous personality transported from Paris by balloon was the Acting Prime Minister Léon Gambetta. The balloon 'Armand-Barbés' was launched on the night of 7 October 1870. The flight ended in an emergency landing in a wood; Gambetta was injured by Prussian bullets, but continued his journey by coach.

The last balloon was launched from the war-ravaged city of Paris on 28 January 1871; it carried on board the Armistice agreement. In total, the balloon post carried eleven tonnes of cargo, most of which was mail, 2.5—3 million letters. Of the 400 carrier pigeons sent out of Paris, only seventy-five returned safely, while none of the five dogs that left the city by balloons succeeded in returning with dispatches as intended. About 100

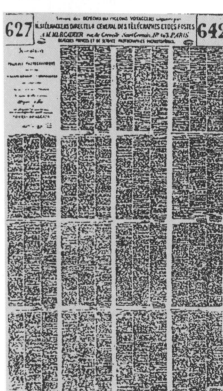

Photographically reduced messages carried to Paris by pigeons.

passengers and sixty-six balloons escaped from Paris, despite Prussian efforts to shoot them down; the arms manufacturer Krupp even designed a special cannon for shooting at airborne targets, which proved ineffective. It is interesting to note that none of the attempts to reach Paris by balloon was successful.

Philatelists at present evaluate the entires transported by balloon posts according to which balloon carried them, where, and when. The number of postal items transported and where the recipients lived also is relevant. Once a balloon landed successfully, its mail would be sorted and forwarded to the recipients in the normal way. From a philatelist's point of view, the entires

delivered to such countries as Malaya, Luxembourg, Canada, and China are considered to be the most valuable.

Before and during the First World War balloons were used to carry mail. Today this is considered classic balloon mail. The modern era of balloon posts has been characterized by their promotion of sporting events and special occasions for which special envelopes, postcards, cachets, souvenir postmarks, and even labels, have been issued. Balloons often have been launched during major philatelic exhibitions as well.

Aircraft Mail

The turn of the 20th century saw the beginning of aircraft transport. Before the First World War, postal administrations and aviation enthusiasts — the latter usually unofficially, and without the approval of the former — be-

gan to explore the suitability of the first aeroplanes for the purpose of carrying mail.

The first official transport of mail by aircraft took place in India, when in January 1911 several flights were operated during the 'United Provinces Industrial and Agricultural' Exhibition at Allahabad. The French pilot H. Pecquet also transported letters and postcards between the Exhibition and the nearest post office. The mail bore a special pre-printed inscription bearing the words 'FIRST AERIAL POST/U.P. EXHIBITION ALLAHABAD, 1911'. The Allahabad post office recorded the handling of this mail with its ordinary postmark. In 1961 the Indian post office issued three commemorative stamps to celebrate the 50th anniversary of this historic event; the stamp with the highest denomination shows the Humber-Sommer biplane, which was used for this first mail flight.

France was second in attempt-

The night launch of a balloon from Paris.

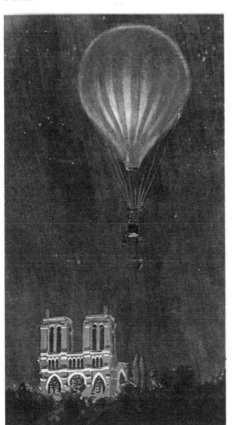

A special postcard transported by balloon from the World Postage Stamp Exhibition 'Praga '88'.

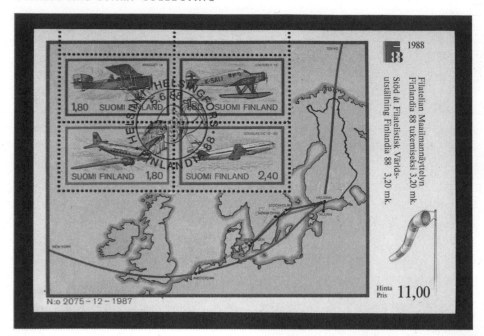

Left: **A commemorative miniature sheet depicting the history of the Finnish airforce.**

Mannheim to Heidelberg on 19 May 1912.

Before the First World War, a number of experimental flights with mail on board took place. This promising co-operation between individual postal administrations and flight enthusiasts was interrupted by the outbreak of hostilities on 28 July 1914. During the War, increasing numbers of planes were manufactured because they were needed for mili-

ing to carry mail by aircraft. On 13 August 1911, the pilot J. Védrines flew from Issay-les-Moulinears to Deauville with a bag of mail aboard his plane.

Great Britain was also among the pioneers of airmail. In September 1911, the United Kingdom Coronation Aerial Post was organized, with flights between London and Windsor. The first flight, of thirty-four kilometres, took place on 9 September and was flown by G. Hamel in a Blériot plane, and lasted only ten minutes. Aboard the plane were 9,000 letters and cards addressed to the King, members at court, ministers, and other important public figures. Further fights took place over the following week because more than 100,000 postal items had to be carried, which the public posted into specially designated aerial letter-boxes throughout London.

The first aircraft carrying mail with the approval of the German postal authorities flew from

Above: **A postcard from the beginnings of airmail in Germany (1912). It was transported by a plane called 'Gelber Hund'.**

Below: **A French monaplane 'Latécoére 28' used to carry mail in the 1920s.**

tary purposes. In 1915 the Austrian post office issued a five-stamp series that depicted the major types of weaponry. The stamp with the highest denomination bore the picture of a reconnaissance plane which was used by the Austrian army.

Even before the end of the First World War, several postal administrations began to carry mail on airship and aircraft that were greatly assisted by advances in technical performance.

The Italian post office issued the first airmail stamps for the Turin–Rome–Turin flight of May 1917, and for the July Naples–Palermo–Naples airship route. A pilot, Bernardini, flew the 530-kilometre-long Turin-Rome route in four hours and three minutes. On board his plane he carried the Turin council's correspondence to the Italian prime minister and the archbishop of Turin's letters to Pope Benedict XV.

Austria also issued airmail stamps for mail carried along routes established before the end of the First World War and the country's collapse. These led primarily from Vienna to Cracow, Lvov and Budapest.

After the end of the War, internal airmail services were introduced to a number of countries. International services were also gradually established. For a few years, however, the use of aircraft was not without problems. While regular airmail services were established, they operated only in the summer months. At this time aeroplanes were not very reliable, and not properly designed to transport large numbers of passengers. As well, the public mistrusted this new means of transport, and thus interna-

Above: A postmark from an airmail post office Berlin C 2 confirming that the letter was transported by air (*top*); a 1930 letter transported on the first flight of the Niort-Paris-Niort route (*bottom*).

Below: A letter transported in 1962 during the first flight of Il-62 on the Prague-Paris route.

tional services dealt mainly with carrying mail. Furthermore, postal administrations could not even guarantee that all mail would be transported by air; in cases where it was not, the airmail surcharge was not refunded.

The development of international airlinks was affected greatly by the international situation. For instance, the then Czechoslovak and British postal authorities signed an agreement that Czechoslovak mail for Great Britain would be flown along the shortest Prague-London route. However, because Germany would not agree to flights over its territory, it had to be flown to Paris, and there transferred on to another flight to London.

In the first months following the War, previous successes of German airship transport inspired their widespread use to carry passengers and cargo on a scale unimaginable for aeroplanes. The Versailles Peace Treaty prohibited Germany from

building airships, however, the 1925 Locarno Treaty permitted further research and the construction of cargo airships; this was fully exploited by Germany.

In addition to Germany, other countries such as Great Britain, the United States, France, Italy, and the former Soviet Union built airships but used them for propaganda and publicity purposes rather than for mail. Only German airships were used regularly for the carriage of mail.

The famous German aviation pioneer Ferdinand von Zeppelin (1838—1917) constructed a number of balloons that could be powered and steered on a predetermined course. The balloons were called 'Zeppelins' after their inventor, and were used to provide regular airlinks. The first ex-

Examples of airmail labels (*from top to bottom*): France, Germany, Sweden, India, New Zealand, Israel, Switzerland, Great Britain, Canada.

The flight of the airship 'Graf Zeppelin'.

perimental mail flights took place in July and August 1909. However, it was only the 'Zeppelin' flights that took place between 1928 and 1937 that became significant in the history of airmail transport. In that period, the 'Zeppelins' carried over forty-nine tonnes of cargo and completed a total of 653 flights; of these, 181 crossed the Atlantic Ocean. Between 1930 and 1934 many countries issued special airmail stamps for the 'Zeppelin'-carried mail.

Most European, and some overseas, postal administrations signed agreements with the German post office concerning mail carried by German airships. These agreements made it possible to cover postage in domestic stamps when mail was transported to South America by the giant airships 'Graf Zeppelin' LZ-127 and the 'Hindenburg' LZ-129. By contrast, mail from nonparticipating countries had to bear German stamps or the stamps of a participating country.

The carriage of mail across the Atlantic Ocean by 'Zeppelins' led to the abolition of the so-called 'catapult post' in 1935. Between the years 1929 and 1935, a few huge transatlantic liners, such as 'Ile-de-France', 'Bremen', and 'Europa' were equipped with catapults for launching aircraft carrying mail from their decks. This meant aircraft could be launched at a distance of up to 1,600 kilometres (1,000 miles) from the nearest port; this facility guaranteed delivery of mail long before the ship actually docked. Such mail was struck with an additional postmark, and today is highly collectable.

Since the Second World War

A letter transported by the 'Graf Zeppelin' to mark the Leipzig fair.

Launching aircraft carrying mail from the liner 'Bremen'.

A postcard carried by an aircraft launched from the liner 'Bremen'.

Aircraft carry tonnes of assorted mail annually.

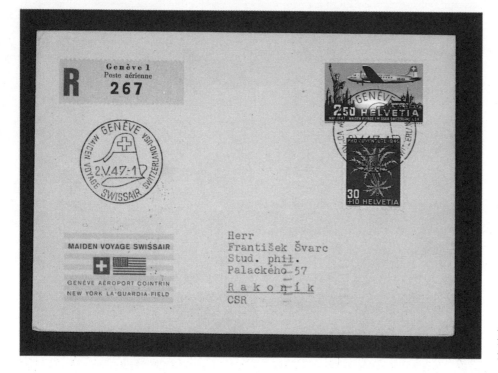

airmail transport has become universal. On domestic routes, mail is transported whenever delivery time can be significantly shortened. This domestic airmail is not specifically identified, and is not liable to a surcharge.

With regard to mail carried overseas, airmail post has greater significance. Mail without an airmail surcharge can still, however, be carried by sea.

Currently, philatelists are interested in inaugural flights on new routes, flights with new types of planes, and anniversary flights operated by various airline companies. Postal administrations sometimes mark these events with special postmarks, and these are usually combined with the airline company's own nonpostal stamp, which is generally made of rubber.

A letter carried in 1947 on the first flight from Geneva to New York (and from there to Czechoslovakia).

10 *The Mail Enters Space*

In the 1930s, Austria's and Germany's attempts to convey mail by rocket were followed by other countries' attempts. While the first intercontinental rockets were also designed to carry mail through space, these attempts did not go beyond the experi-

A Czechoslovak miniature sheet marking the flight of the Soviet 'Vega' spacecraft, which was launched to investigate the planet Venus, and Halley's Comet. Some of its equipment was provided by France and several Intercosmos member states.

American and Soviet stamps issued to mark the experimental 'Soyuz-Apollo' flight.

mental stage. In 1939 the Cuban post office even issued a special stamp to mark these experiments, as did the Mexican post office in 1961.

The United States' first attempt to transport mail by spacecraft took place in February 1962. The venture was privately sponsored, and mail was to be transported on board the spacecraft 'Friendship 7'. Envelopes were franked with the fifteen-cent airmail stamp and cancelled at Cape Canaveral. The cancellation inscription stated that the astronaut John Glenn carried the envelope

Commemorative stamps issued to mark the launch of the first French satellite 'A 1'.

into space; however Glenn refused to take mail, and even struck out the inscription on one envelope. This envelope is currently exhibited in the space flight archive in Amsterdam.

An interesting experiment was carried out earlier in September 1960, which was part of 'Discoverer', an American space-research programme dealing with the recovery of items from orbit in space. A 'space letter' was franked with a seven-cent airmail stamp and cancelled by the postmark of a small Californian post office. The envelope also bore the inscription SATELLITE MAIL. When the rocket had orbited the earth three times, the case with the enclosed letter was ejected, and then recovered from the air by aeroplane. The letter had travelled six-and-one-half million kilometres in space, at a speed of 16,000 kilometres-per-hour. This space experiment, although rather unsophisticated, is significant in postal history.

Space Postmasters

Space post took its first real steps in January 1969 when the two Soviet spaceships 'Soyuz 4' and 'Soyuz 5' docked in space. When 'Soyuz 5's cosmonauts boarded 'Soyuz 4', carrying mail with them, they in fact became the first space postmen. They handed the mail over to 'Soyuz 4's cosmonauts. The mail consisted of newspapers and letters from the launch centre director, other cosmonauts, families, and well-wishers. Live television pictures of this historic event were transmitted to earth. The director's letter was enclosed in an envelope that bore the inscription COSMIC POST. The envelope had an impressed Soviet stamp of the most common denomination — the four-*kopeck* stamp — and was cancelled with an EARTH—COSMOS —COSMOS—EARTH date-stamp picturing a spacecraft, and bearing the date 14 January 1969.

The United States postal administration carried out a similar experiment during the 'Apollo 11' spacecraft mission to the Moon. The astronauts took with them an envelope with an imprinted 'Moon letter' stamp and the die of a future American Moon-landing commemorative stamp. According to a carefully planned brief, this new stamp, with its inscription, FIRST MAN ON THE MOON, UNITED STATES, was to be launched symbolically on the Moon. The astronauts Neil Armstrong and Edwin Aldrin were to imitate 'a lunar post office' by stamping the letter with a special MOON LAND-ING JULY 20 1969, USA, handstamp.

The astronauts did indeed raise the 'Stars and Stripes' on the moon; they also carried out their planned research programme, but the envelope, the die of the future stamp, and the commemorative handstamp remained in the lunar module cabin. The astronauts only remembered their 'postmaster' roles on the return journey to earth. They struck the rubber date-stamp on to the envelope; they did not use the die of the new stamp at all. This cancelled 'Moon letter' was handed over to the United States postal administration after the three-week quarantine period which the crew and cargo had to undergo. The die itself, however, was subject to a speedy disinfection, and on 31 July 1969 it was transported by special plane to Washington D.C. On 9 September

A book of stamps issued by the Mauritian post office to commemorate the 'Apollo' spacecraft's landing on the Moon.

The first man
on the Moon,
Neil Armstrong.

An American
stamp
commemorat-
ing the 'First
Man on the
Moon'.

and a stamp-pad were carefully wrapped up and placed inside the lunar vehicle. A similar envelope was placed on board the orbiting 'Apollo 15' module, which waited for the return of the two astronauts who had landed on the Moon.

Once on the moon, astronaut Scott cancelled the postal administration's envelope with the special MOON LANDING, AUG. 2 1971, USA stamp, which millions of people were able to watch live on television. However, it was later discovered that the astronaut had left the hand-stamp on the moon. Fortunately, this envelope was not the only one cancelled on the moon's surface, as the astronauts privately cancelled a further 400 letters. In addition to these, a further 250 letters remained in the orbiting 'Apollo 15' module.

These examples represent the first stages in the development of space post. In order to make 'space letters' acceptable as official postal items, further experiments have since been undertaken. However, so far none of these has complied with the UPU regulations. To meet these regulations, postal administrations would have to set up 'space postal rates' and to issue 'space stamps'. No doubt both of these will be common occurrences in our grandchildren's lifetimes.

the new stamp went on sale at the Capitol's main post office. The 'Moon letter' and the die are now on permanent display in the United States postal administration's exhibition hall.

The second 'lunar' postal event is linked with the 'Apollo 15' spacecraft flight of 1971. The United States postal administration asked that the National Aeronautics and Space Administration (NASA) transport an envelope franked with the latest United States space stamp to the moon, together with a cancelling stamp. The proposal was accepted. An experimental stamp proof consisting of two specimens was struck, perforated by hand, and finally affixed to the envelope. The envelope, the rubber stamp,

11 *Thematic Philately*

The first stamps were primarily of postal significance because philatelists and stamp collecting did not yet exist. These early stamps were postal papers, which often depicted symbols of state power, such as a portrait of a sovereign, or a national coat-of-arms. Those countries which had a republican form of government — such as the United States and the French Republic of 1852 — would occasionally portray presidents on their stamps or they would use various allegories or ancient mythological figures.

Postage stamps on the topic of music.

Simple numerical motifs were also common in some countries, such as Brazil, Saxony, or the Swiss canton of Zürich.

Towards the end of the 19th century, some postal administrations realized that the illustration on a stamp could also be used to promote the issuing country. This led to the issue of the first special stamps, which became more prominent after the First World War.

The practice of issuing such

Examples of stamps for a specialized stamp collection 'Europe' and the 'Red Cross'.

stamps has become common since 1945, and has created conditions for the rise of thematic philately, which took several decades to establish itself fully. Unlike traditional philately, it is the stamp illustration or its motif that matters in thematic philately. Its development since the Second World War was a consequence of the appearance of various stamp issues all over the world; there is almost no sphere of human activity that is not depicted on postage stamps.

Thematic and Subject Philately

This new branch of philately initially developed as subject philately. The philatelist would compile his collection and exhibits from stamps bearing similar or related subjects, or stamps that were issued for the same reason

Postage stamps on the topic of sport.

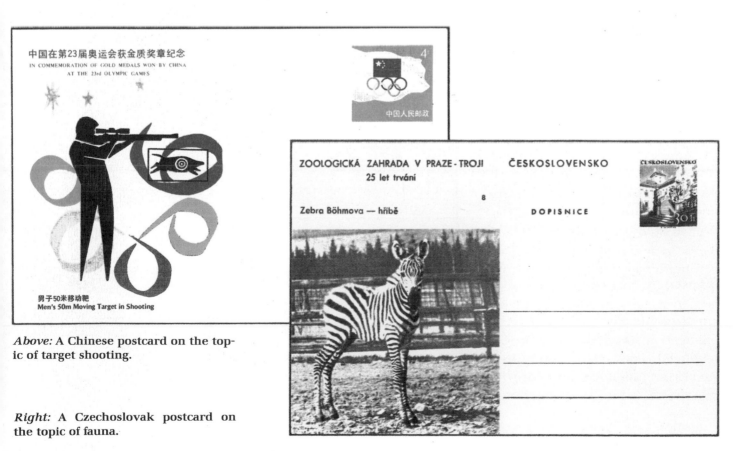

Above: A Chinese postcard on the topic of target shooting.

Right: A Czechoslovak postcard on the topic of fauna.

Postage stamps on the topic of fauna.

or purpose. For instance, a collection concerned with the Red Cross would concentrate on those stamps depicting the Red Cross symbol. In addition to the symbol, however, these stamps — usually charity stamps with a surtax designed to benefit the Red Cross — might bear a symbolic design or portray a cultural monument. In this way the picture on a stamp might only rarely be related to Red Cross activities.

This somewhat mechanical arranging of postage stamps, although related to a chosen topic, soon lost its attractiveness in the eyes of many collectors. Gradually, thematic grouping, which is prevalent today, gained ground. The purpose of this type of collecting is to document and illustrate a selected theme not only with stamps but also with special cancellations, postal papers, and other related philatelic material.

Anyone wishing to compile a Red Cross thematic collection will try to show the history and reasons for the establishment of the Red Cross, the personality of its founder and those who have promoted its development, and its main activities, such as assistance to prisoners-of-war. In addition to stamps, whose subject illustrates a chosen topic, the collector will also assemble postal items that document Red Cross activities, such as prisoner-of-war correspondence that was exchanged through the Red Cross, or postal cards documenting the Red Cross-initiated search for soldiers reported missing in action.

Portrait de modèle (1878 - 1880)

132

Postage stamps relating to the creative arts.

Left: August Renoir's painting 'Model', together with postage stamp and commemorative postmark.

Post Office and Thematic Philately

Over the years, philatelists' enthusiasm has led to their increased demands for perfection: they may no longer be satisfied with a stamp depicting the chosen theme symbolically, be it a plant, a tree, a car, a rocket, or an animal. They request that the stamp should illustrate a specific kind, type, or model, which will enable them to illustrate more precisely certain sub-topics of their collection. Collectors often become very knowledgeable about a certain period of postal history, postal cancellations, or postal papers. Needless to say, they are experts in the field that they have chosen for the theme of their collections.

Postal administrations take philatelists' interests into account when issuing new stamps, simultaneously publishing information that may assist thematic collectors. This information, in an abridged form, finds its way into philatelic magazines and stamp catalogues. However, the collector has still to establish many facts, and so some philatelic societies have specialized sections just for thematic collectors.

12 The Creation of a Postage Stamp

From Design to Print

Initially, a postal administration's stamp-issuing department will compile a stamp list, which is done with consideration for forthcoming state anniversaries, significant events, and proposals submitted by various agencies. As mentioned previously, stamps are not just proof of prepaid postage, but also have great promotional and propaganda functions when affixed to postal items, which may be conveyed around the world.

Once the issue list has been approved, postal administrations often hold competitions for individual stamp designs, or they might simply entrust graphic designers with the task. The designer will be provided with the necessary information concerning the stamp's theme, the proposed format, the number of colours that are to be used, the suggested printing technique, and the appropriate texts and nominative values. Sometimes a photograph is offered as guidance to the stamp's subject.

Recess printing is the most complicated and the most advanced printing technique used in stamp production today. It relies significantly on both the printer's experience and the artist's graphic skills.

The graphic artist has an unenviable task: to create a work that combines artistic qualities with the utility and propaganda functions of a postal paper. He or she will usually prepare a number of designs, which are then scaled-up several times larger than the stamp's actual size. The design will be evaluated and assessed by a selection panel, which is the postal administration's advisory body.

Eminent stamp designers: a 1903 Canadian stamp with the bust of King Edward VII was designed by R. J. A. Tilleard and the future King George V (1910—1936). Franz Jonas (1899—1974), an Austrian president, and a 1965 stamp which he designed to commemorate the 50th anniversary of the Austrian town union. A miniature sheet issued to mark a stamp exhibition 'PhilexFrance 82' portrays Marianne de Cocteau, a drawing by Jean Cocteau (1898—1963).

Examples of stamps designed by children: Czechoslovakia, Great Britain, Argentina, Bulgaria.

Dutch stamps depicting computer-designed drawings from 1970.

An engraver working on a postage stamp.

The designs have to be laid out in lines. If executed differently, the designer or the engraver will be asked to prepare the so-called 'linear drawing'. An engraver will incise the mirror-image of the design on to a copper or a steel plate. His task is as important as the designer's. In addition, he may have to adapt the design to correspond to the stamp's actual dimensions. Simultaneously, he attempts to capture the given subject as realistically as possible. Looking through a magnifying glass, the engraver works with a tool called a graver. He incises the stamp design on to a plate, fully aware that the engraved lines cannot be corrected easily; at the same time, he has to employ all of his professional skills and display all of his artistic sensitivity.

Transferring a stamp's illustration from the original plate on to a malette.

First Day Covers issued by postal authorities in the US, Sweden, and Switzerland. They are a special type of entire issued by many postal authorities, but also by stamp dealers, on the first day of validity of a new stamp or a new stamp issue. The covers usually have a drawing or text relevant to the stamp topic on the left of the address side; they bear a first-day cancellation.

Once the engraver has completed the design in metal — the die — another complicated operation follows in which a large printing plate with a specified number of stamps is prepared. The original engraved steel plate is hardened to withstand great pressure. It is then clamped to a matrix punching press, together with a small steel roller called a malette. In this way, the design is transferred to the malette, which is hardened, and the process is repeated.

Next, a specified number of stamps is impressed on to a large printing plate or on to a printing roller. The metal on to which stamp designs are transferred responds to pressure, and raised surfaces appear at the side of each future stamp. These have to be filed carefully so that the

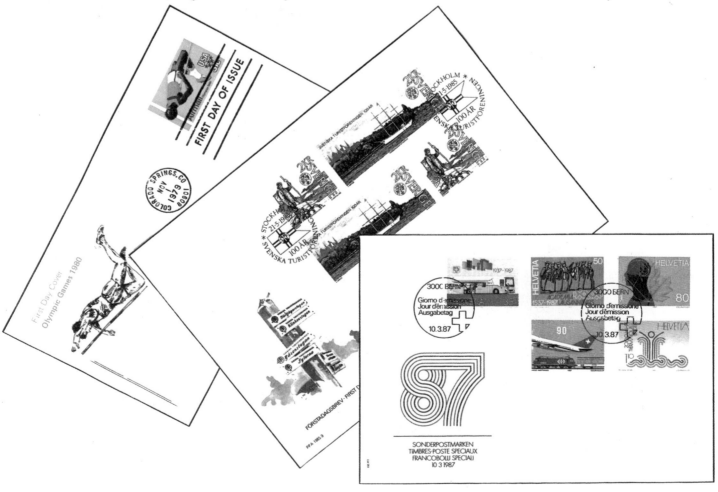

A printing roller impressed with a specified number of stamp designs using a malette.

Johann Gutenberg, the inventor of typographic printing.

plate's or roller's surface becomes smooth. The printing plate or the roller is immersed in a galvanic bath, which prevents a rapid wearing off. If the stamp is to be multicoloured, separate engravings and also printing plates must be made for each of the colours. Generally, the

stamp appears as several million specimens.

The Principal Methods of Stamp Printing

During the 150 years that stamps have been issued, they have been printed by various processes. While some printing techniques can be recognized immediately, others cannot, especially if various techniques are applied during the production of a particular stamp. For the purposes of this book, it will be sufficient if the principal printing techniques used in the past and at present are mentioned briefly.

In general, the techniques of relief printing, planographic printing, and recess, or intaglio, printing can all be used for stamp production.

Relief printing involves transferring coloured inks from raised surfaces on the printing plate. The hollow surfaces do not absorb colour, and remain 'blank' on the paper. The use of a simple rubber stamp is an example of relief printing. The most commonly used and most important type of relief printing is typographic printing, invented by Johann Gutenberg (c. 1400–1468).

When the manual and machine compositions were in use, the term 'typographic printing' in its narrowest sense meant the printing of books and newspapers. However, in philately the term stands for any kind of relief printing, and it is commonly used in stamp catalogues. The original technique of typographic printing was not suitable for reproducing pictures, and especially was not suitable for stamp production because the design was repeated

a hundred times or more per sheet. The stamp design would therefore first be engraved into metal (usually copper), and a printing form or a plate was prepared using galvanized dies. The philatelist can distinguish a relief-produced mint stamp by identifying that the imprinted design is slightly embossed into the stamp paper. Convex surfaces on the stamp reverse are also evidence of this. In the 19th century typographic printing was used for stamp production in many countries such as Great Britain, France, Austria, and Switzerland. It has also been used in this century in Spain, Czechoslovakia, and Italy.

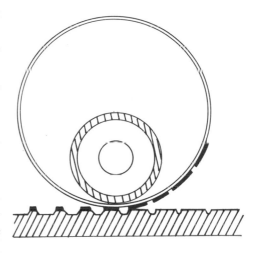

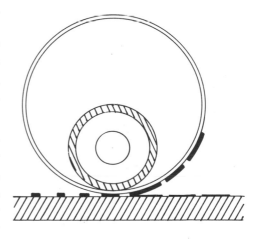

A diagram of typographic printing (top) and a diagram of planographic printing (above).

137

Alois Senefelder, the inventor of lithography.

Planographic printing, whether from a printing plate or from a cylinder, depends on the printing and non-printing surfaces being even. This is also the principle employed by special printing techniques, the oldest of which is lithography, which was discovered in 1796 by Alois Senefelder (1771—1834), a native of Prague. A special stone, so-called lithographic stone, made of fine grained limestone is prepared in such a way that those surfaces of the stone that are to transfer the design accept oily printing ink while other surfaces reject it.

Lithography was used for printing stamps, especially in the last century, by Hungary, Argentina, Venezuela, and China. Stamps printed by this technique have designs without any embossed surfaces on the front side, and without any convex surfaces on the reverse. Ink is laid on thinly, but when magnified it is evident that it is not distributed evenly. The designs of lithographic stamps look less sophisticated, less distinct, and less fine than other printing techniques. The outlines and lines are often interrupted and fine lines look shaky. In contrast to typographic printing, for which it is often mistaken, lithography is lacking in distinct outlines.

The most advanced type of planographic printing is offset printing. This is in fact a technically developed form of lithography. The difference between the two is that smooth stone plates are replaced by zinc or aluminium plates that are clamped to a rotary press machine-roller. From the metal plate the inked design is first transferred on to a rubber cylinder, and then on to the paper. Printing is much faster when the rotary method is used. For each colour, a separate printing plate must be prepared. Modern rotary press machines have these plates arranged next to one another or above one another, so that a paper 'web' going through the system of rollers has colours printed in succession. Offset printing has been used to print stamps in Austria, Turkey, Germany, and the former Soviet Union.

Recess (intaglio) printing is based on a different principle from relief printing. Printing elements are engraved on to the surface of the printing plate or the roller, and printing ink, which fills incised or etched places of different depressions, is transferred on to the printed material. The main recess printing techniques are die-stamping, copperplate printing, and photogravure, which is one of the most widespread modern printing techniques.

Die-stamping was used for printing the first British stamps of 1840–1841. It is still used by the postal administrations of the United States, France and Canada. Copperplate printing was used to produce the first Belgian stamps of 1849–1863.

Photogravure is a printing technique invented by the Czech painter Karel Klíč (1841–1926). It involves transferring a photograph on to a copper plate, which is covered with specks of the finest asphalt. The plate is then etched, and various depressions appear depending on the degree

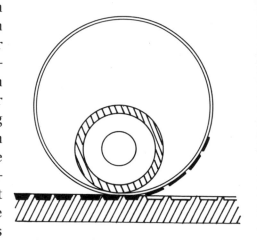

A diagram of intaglio printing.

Karel Klíč, the inventor of photogravure, depicted on a Czechoslovak stamp.

is also used to print stamps in France, the former Soviet Union, and Mexico.

In addition to offset printing and die-stamping, at present screen printing has been most commonly used in stamp production. Postal administrations, however, do not restrict themselves to the exclusive use of one printing technique; some stamps are even produced using a printing process, such as die-stamping combined with offset, or die-stamping combined with screen printing.

A 1972 stamp issued by the West Berlin post depicts rotary recess printing of a stamp.

of light. As the asphalt specks capture light, they create an especially fine tone to the design, which cannot be achieved by any other printing technique. During a stay in London, Klíč improved this technique by replacing the asphalt layer with numerous tiny squares formed by a meshed screen on the printed surface of a photograph, a method that today is known as 'screen printing'. At present, most British stamps are printed by this technique; it

13 *Forgeries, Forgers, and Experts*

Art or Forgery?

Postage stamp forgeries are nearly as old as their originals. They appeared in the 1850s in order to defraud the post by forging commonly used stamps for covering postage. As there were no philatelists to examine stamps carefully, it usually took some time to identify a postal forgery, that is, a forgery made to defraud the post office.

One postal forgery, which had been carried out successfully for several years in Britain, was discovered only accidentally. In 1870, the British post office took over the administration of the telegraph service, which had been operated privately until then. The postal rate for a twenty-word wire was set at one shilling. The postal clerk would acknowledge the payment by affixing a one-shilling stamp on the reverse of the wire form, which was retained for several years as evidence in case of complaints. After the prescribed time, bundles of old wires were sent to paper mills for recycling.

In 1898, a mill employee broke the regulations and sold some bundles of wire forms dating from 1871–1872 to a stamp dealer. The dealer carefully removed the postage stamps from the reverse of the wire forms and began to sell them. Philatelists soon became interested in these one-shilling stamps, however, when they examined them and compared them to similar stamps of the period, they discovered flaws and errors. Primarily, the stamps lacked watermarks, and the designs were not well executed. The philatelic press voiced their suspicions that these stamps had been postal forgeries. The post office ordered an investigation, which revealed that all the suspicious specimens had come from a certain counter at the London stock exchange. Over the years, the British post office had been defrauded of the then huge sum of £15,000. Postal records were used to identify the clerk who had worked at this counter. He had since retired, lived in a small house and was enjoying his pension. The post office was unable to prosecute him because there was no evidence that he had forged the stamps in question. The forger remains unknown to this day.

Postal forgeries used on entires are extremely popular among collectors, while collectors' forgeries, which are made to defraud collectors, are worthless as philatelic material. Such forgeries imitate highly priced or very rare stamps, which are then offered to collectors either as genuine stamps or their cheaper facsimiles. A collectors' forgery may be either complete or partial. In the latter case, only a part of the original is forged, that is, an overprint is forged on a genuine stamp; a postal cancellation is forged.

Towards the end of the 1890s, Sigmund Friedl, a well-known

An example of forged perforation. The remnants of the original perforation are still visible.

A primitive forgery of numerical obliteration. The forger changed a single-digit number into a double-digit number.

Viennese stamp dealer, happened to discover a large number of rare yellow, pink, and vermilion 'Mercuries'. This caused astonishment and aroused a great deal of interest among collectors. 'Mercuries' are the world's first newspaper stamps, issued in 1851 by Austria. They take their name from the Roman god Mercury, the protector of roads and travellers, who is depicted on these stamps. Because their denominations were not given, the stamps differed in colour. The blue stamp was used to frank one newspaper copy; the yellow stamp franked ten copies; the pink stamp franked fifty copies. In 1856, yellow 'Mercuries' were replaced by the more striking vermilion stamps.

These yellow, pink, and vermilion 'Mercuries' are valuable stamps because they were issued in relatively small numbers. Furthermore, publishers would dispatch ten or more newspapers tied with an addressed wrapper to which a stamp was affixed.

In most cases, the recipient would throw away the wrapper with its cancelled stamp. Thus, only seven used specimens and 30 to 40 mint specimens have been preserved out of the 120,000

vermilion 'Mercuries' issued.

This may help to explain the huge interest among collectors in Sigmund Friedl's discovery. Friedl quickly sold the 'Mercuries' he had uncovered, and soon afterwards came across more specimens. A further discovery followed, and philatelists began to grow suspicious. Indeed, concrete evidence was soon published showing that the 'Mercuries' on sale were forgeries. Friedl, however, rejected all

these suspicions. As he was a reputable stamp dealer, he was able to claim that a campaign was being waged againts him. However, when the Vienna mint decreed that the stamps had indeed been forgeries, Friedl had to refund all the purchasers, close up his business, and retire. This is just one story of many collectors' forgeries.

Jean Baptiste Moens (1833–1908), a Belgian philatelist and a stamp dealer, is one of the first acknowledged forgers. It is an interesting coincidence that Moens also published a work entitled *De la falsification des timbres-poste* ('Forging Postage Stamps'). Its author was Louis François Hançiau, one of the earliest Belgian philatelists.

Moens bought surplus Belgian definitive stamps of 1849–1863 that were invalidated by a red ink line. He chemically removed the ink cancellation, and sold these stamps as mint specimens.

The First Postal Paper Exhibition held in Vienna in November 1881 was attended by many important stamp dealers. Sigmund Friedl, a Viennese dealer, had his stall on the rear left.

He also had proofs and reprints of the German state of Bergendorf printed, and sold them too. A reprint is a copy of the original printing issue, now invalid, which is officially issued for propaganda and promotional purposes. Moens' reprints and proofs were unofficial, and therefore have to be considered forgeries.

Many forgers have become 'philatelic celebrities' when their exceptionally well-executed forgeries have finally been uncovered. If the forger himself is an expert in his specialized area of philately, and is equipped with the appropriate technical and material means, such as the stamp paper and inks, he is invariably able to produce excellent and damaging forgeries. However, long experience shows that anyone who is well acquainted with the original stamps is almost certain to detect such forgeries.

The case of the forgeries of François Fournier (1846–1917) is one example of how even a technically well-equipped printing company could not produce forgeries that would deceive a vigilant expert. Fournier became the owner of a small Swiss printing company that had been established in 1891 by L. H. Mercier, a producer of 'art imitations', a term Mercier used when referring to his complete and partial forgeries of various early philatelic rarities. Fournier continued in his activity; in addition his company began to issue a magazine that promoted the idea that it was preferable to have a facsimile stamp than an empty space in a stamp album. In this way Fournier excused his forgeries, and proclaimed how harmless his illegal venture was. Thanks to the benevolent nature of the contemporary Swiss law, he did not have to fear any prosecution.

When Fournier died the printing company became less prosperous. When the new owner died in 1927, it was necessary to resolve what to do with the large stock of complete and partial forgeries, and how to dispose of the printing equipment. The Geneva Philatelic Society realized the possible threat to collectors, and decided to purchase the whole estate and acquaint the philatelic public with its nature. The Society compiled 475 stamp album that provided samples of all types of Fournier's forgeries: forged stamps, overprints, and cancellations which were now distinctly marked as forgeries. Steps were also taken to prevent further misuse of the printing material to produce new forgeries by donating it to the Geneva Museum.

A Master Forger

Only today can a philatelic expert equipped with the latest technical tools recognize Sperati's stamp forgeries, some of the best-ever executed. Jean de Sperati (1884–1957), an Italian painter and engraver who lived in southern France, was an exceptionally knowledgeable printing expert, an accomplished chemist, an artist — and a master forger. His forgeries of several hundred rare classical stamps were so masterfully executed that their design, colour, and paper can only be distinguished from the original issues when magnified and examined under a testing lamp — and even then with the greatest difficulty.

Sperati never tried to sell his work as genuine postage stamps, but sold them as 'art reproductions' at a fraction of the cost of the genuine stamps. With each of his stamps he provided a certificate that recorded that the stamp was an imitation. He would not, however, mark his reproductions in any recognizable way, and would not of course give any guarantee that they might never be misused.

Aged seventy-two and prevented from further work by his failing eyesight, Sperati retired and sold the rest of his forgeries to

A Belgian stamp issued to commemorate the 50th Anniversary of the Belgian Stamp Dealers' Association. It depicts Jean Baptiste Moens (1833–1908), one of the most important 19th-century stamp dealers.

Examples of François Fournier's forging tools, today in the Geneva Museum.

the British Philatelic Federation. It was only then that philatelists realized how damaging the facsimiles were, and suspicions about the originality of several world rarities were voiced. The British Philatelic Federation came up with the idea of exhibiting these forgeries and publishing 500 copies of their album to sell to its members and the members of the Royal Philatelic Society. This met with a certain apprehension, but caused huge interest among British philatelists. The Federation carried out its scheme. The whole affair is all the more significant as it does not date from the beginnings of philately, but took place in 1957, shortly before Sperati's death.

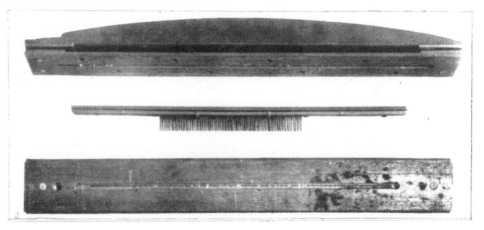

Wartime Forgeries

Stamp forgeries intended for military and sabotage purposes form a special group that is of great interest to collectors. Such forgeries appeared during both World Wars. Generally speaking, they are stamp forgeries issued by a political and military enemy, which are either indistinguishable from their originals and

serve to be passed off as originals, or are printed with certain variations for the purposes of propaganda.

During the First World War, forgeries of German and Bavarian stamps were produced by Great Britain. Allied agents used these stamps to cover postage on leaflets and propaganda materials delivered throughout Germany or on the German Front by the German post office. When occupying the Rhineland, French soldiers used these stamps to frank their private correspondence. Forgeries of Austrian stamps were also produced to serve similar purposes.

During the Second World War, forgeries of British stamps were produced in the concentration camp Oranienburg-Sachsenhausen. These too were issued for German propaganda purposes so that, for example, the stamp bearing the portrait of the British King George VI was slightly altered, and his crown was embellished with the Star of David; another stamp bore a hammer and sickle in place of its nominative value.

In 1944 the American military press issued the six-pfennig and twelve-pfennig German stamps in Rome. These stamps bore the inscription Futsches Reich instead of Deutsches Reich, and Hitler was portrayed as a skeleton. Other examples of similar forgeries are in existence.

Protection Against Forgeries

To safeguard itself against forgery, the British post office printed special corner letters on early British stamps.

The Prussian post selected another method of protection. The Prussian postage stamps with the portrait of King Friedrich Wilhelm IV (1795–1861) are among the best graphical specimens of that time, with fine engraving simultaneously combined with a design of classical simplicity. The stamps are without any unnecessary embellishments. The second issue was protected against forgery by a meshed network of lead oxide, which was in-

Below, left and right: **Samples from an album of Sperati's forgeries.**

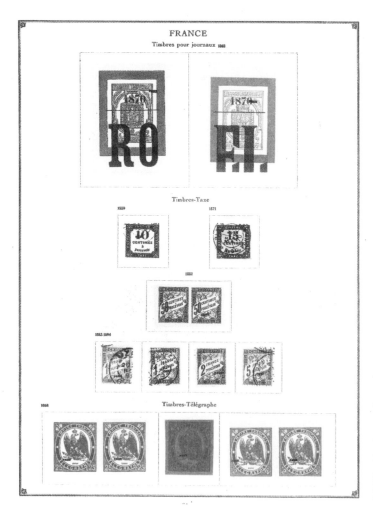

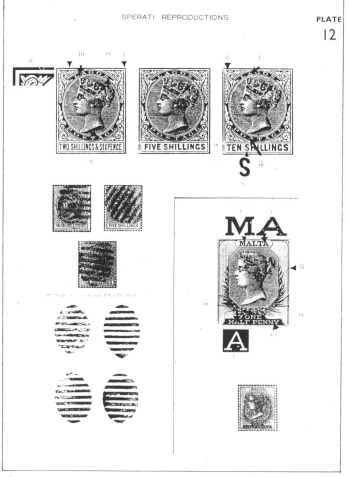

144

Forging stamps in Nazi concentration camp Sachsenhausen: a) a British stamp with a portrait of King George VI (1936–1952) — a German forgery of the same stamp (*above*); b) the 1937 stamp issued to mark King George VI's accession to the throne — a forgery (*below*); c) a special stamp issued to mark 25 years of King George V (1910–1936) rule — a forgery (*below*).

visible to the naked eye. The network would only become visible if the stamp was dipped into a weak solution of hydrogen sulphide, which would result in a blackish or brownish colour appearing on the stamp. This test was designed purely for postal purposes. It is not known whether any collector ever decided to put his stamps to this test.

The first Japanese stamps, which were issued in 1871–1872, portrayed two heraldic dragons, the symbol of the ruling dynasty. This dragon symbol appeared on all state documents, and its unauthorized use and imitation was punishable by death. However, not even this penalty could safeguard Japanese stamps from being forged. Compared to the present day, these Japanese stamps were issued in relatively small numbers, and were soon greatly in demand. This might have been one reason for their forgery. The stamps were beautifully engraved. In addition to the two dragons, the engravers succeeded in including both a rich ornamental design and the

stamp's nominal value in an elaborate structure. Any potential forgers had to be gifted artists and skilled craftsmen, like the original engravers.

Whole sheets of these much sought-after stamps soon appeared in some Japanese towns, especially in ports. Forgers were aware of the mandatory capital punishment if caught, and were therefore not interested in their forged stamps entering the public domain, as that would have increased the risk of detection. They preferred to sell their forged stamps in ports to departing foreigners who would take them abroad.

In addition, Japanese forgers marked all their work as forgeries. They included tiny symbols and hoped that this might earn them more lenient treatment if they were discovered by the authorities. Foreigners could hardly discern these miniature symbols at first glance. Even if they did notice them under a magnifying glass, they would naturally presume that they were part of the stamp's design.

Watermarked paper already existed in the pre-stamp period, and today, as then, is the most common means of protection against forgery. Watermarked paper is also used for the manufacture of banknotes.

Originally the watermark was created during the paper manufacturing process. A filter, which served for draining water from the manufactured paper stock, had a meshed bottom with interwoven ornaments, trademarks, or wire patterns, the so-called 'filigrees'. The layer of paper stock became thinner and transparent in these places, thus preserving the shape of ornaments and filigrees. This design served as both the manufacturer's guarantee and an embellishment. Imitating a watermark is impossible, and it therefore began to be used as protection against forgery.

In recent years, printing techniques used in stamp manufacture have been greatly improved, and watermarked paper has lost some of its importance. It is still being used, partly in order to maintain a long tradition, and partly to make stamps more attractive to collectors.

Today, postal forgeries are less common than in the past because modern printing techniques make them more difficult. Forgers focus instead on producing facsimiles of the more valuable stamps to sell to collectors. For example, cheaper genuine stamps are used to produce forgeries by chemically altering colour, by overprinting, or by altering perforations.

The Expert at Work

The Belgian philatelist Louis François Hançiau, mentioned previously, can be considered the forefather of all postage stamp experts. Present-day criteria for considering someone to be a philatelic expert are more demanding than in the past. The expert

The microscope, an important tool in the hands of a stamp expert. It helps to establish the composition of stamp paper.

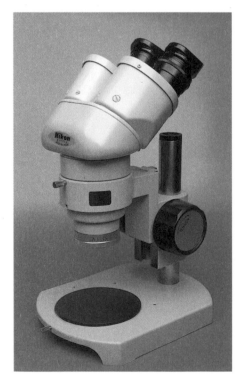

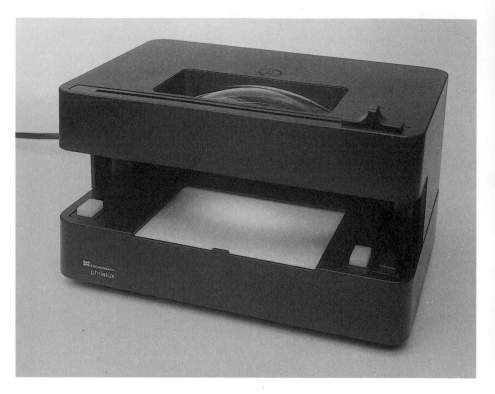

An ultraviolet lamp is indispensable when trying to differentiate colours, which may look the same in daylight. It helps to establish various stamp issues. It can discover minute repairs to stamps. The illustrated lamp can also be used as a microscope because it can magnify objects.

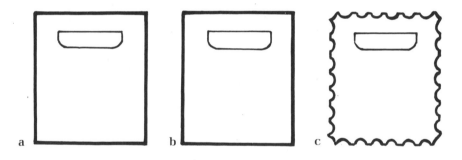

Examples of placing a control mark: a) on a genuine mint unperforated stamp; b) on a genuine used unperforated badly damaged stamp; c) on a genuine mint perforated stamp.

must know the original stamp and all its variants intimately. Practically speaking, the expert has to be a specialist who has mastered a specific area of collecting; he must be well acquainted with the different printing techniques and the production and usage of stamps; he must be able to carry out a scrupulous examination of stamps with reference to perforation, stamp paper, and other criteria. He must also have at his disposal all the philatelic reference literature relevant to his collecting interest; he must possess the appropriate technical equipment and comparative philatelic material in his own collection, or at least have access to originals in other collections. He must also have a certain philatelic sixth sense as he cannot know everything about stamps.

The expert masters his area, which may embrace one stamp-

150 LET POŠTOVNÍ ZNÁMKY
150 YEARS OF THE POSTAGE STAMP

One of the miniature sheets issued to commemorate the 150th anniversary of the world's first postage stamps.

issuing country in total, or one particular period — perhaps one issue or one stamp only — or several stamp-issuing countries in total, or a part of their stamp issues, such as airmail stamps of several countries.

When examining a particular stamp, the expert applies a set of criteria, that is, he checks step-by-step for the signs of authenticity. Even if only one sign is lacking, the stamp under review will certainly be a forgery.

The expert places his mark on the reverse of the stamp. It usual-ly consists of a miniature stamp, signed or marked by a cipher. This testifies that the stamp in question is, for example, perfor-ated or unperforated; with or without an overprint; damaged or slightly damaged; used or can-celled. If the stamp is a complete forgery, the expert will record this on the stamp reverse by writ-ing FORGERY or FAUX. If the stamp is a partial forgery, the expert will record what has been forged, for example FORGED OVERPRINT.

The position of the expert's mark on the stamp's reverse is set by an international custom. Perforated stamps have the ex-pert's mark positioned differently from unperforated stamps. Sim-ilarly, stamps with and without an overprint differ as to the posi-tion of the expert's mark. This is to prevent alterations of perforat-ed stamps into unperforated ones; or the forging of stamps originally without an overprint into stamps with a forged over-print. The quality of the stamp is also reflected in the positioning of the expert's mark; less valu-able stamps have the expert's mark further up from the stamp's bottom edge.

However, the mark of one ex-pert or of several reputable ex-perts does not provide a fully re-liable guarantee that the stamp is genuine. It has to be remember-ed that the forger who can pro-duce a fine stamp will also be able to forge the expert's mark.

Philatelists are aware of certain cases in which a collector has been offered a valuable stamp, whose authenticity has been vouched for on its reverse by the marks of two philatelic experts — and indeed, both the stamp and the experts' marks have been forged. It is therefore sensible when buying or exchanging a rare stamp that has the expert's mark on the reverse to ask for a second opinion. Furthermore, the quality of the stamp was re-corded only at the time of its ex-amination, and could have been damaged subsequently.

Conclusion

When it was first suggested that postage stamps be introduced for public use in the 1850s, no one could have imagined that this innovation would simplify postal operations significantly, open up new possibilities for the development of postal systems, and result in the appearance of a new collecting activity known as philately. Neither Rowland Hill nor his predecessors could ever have guessed that stamp collecting would command such widespread interest. It has captured the minds of many people, young and old alike; important artists have participated in stamp production; and the quality and standard of stamps have witnessed the technical competence of each stamp-issuing country.

The world of philately will continue to grow and change, reflecting mankind's interests, hopes, and desires. As long as there are stamps, there always will be philatelists to collect and enjoy them.

INDEX